Elizabeth M Robertson *(NHS Grampian, UK)*

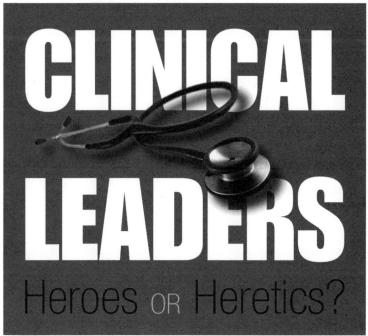

CLINICAL LEADERS

Heroes OR Heretics?

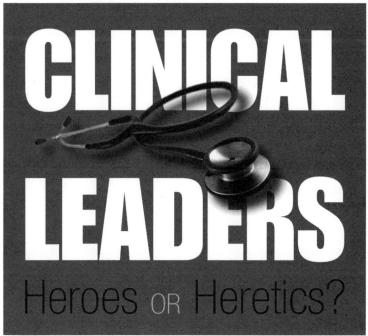

World Scientific

NEW JERSEY · LONDON · SINGAPORE · BEIJING · SHANGHAI · HONG KONG · TAIPEI · CHENNAI

Published by

World Scientific Publishing Co. Pte. Ltd.

5 Toh Tuck Link, Singapore 596224

USA office: 27 Warren Street, Suite 401-402, Hackensack, NJ 07601

UK office: 57 Shelton Street, Covent Garden, London WC2H 9HE

British Library Cataloguing-in-Publication Data
A catalogue record for this book is available from the British Library.

CLINICAL LEADERS
Heroes or Heretics?

ISBN-13 978-981-4299-83-1
ISBN-10 981-4299-83-9

Typeset by Stallion Press
Email: enquiries@stallionpress.com

Printed in Singapore by World Scientific Printers.

Dedication

I dedicate this to those, working with whom,
have inspired me to write the book.

More personally I dedicate the book to my mother,
Dorothy Robertson, who has always supported
and encouraged my endeavours.

Acknowledgements

My grateful thanks to David Benton who read and commented on early drafts of the book and Kay MacKenzie who went through the text with great care helping with clarity of understanding and grammar. Both encouraged and helped me.

Contents

Why? By Way of a Foreword!

Why is there a need for this book or why is there a need for clinical leadership?

Clinical leadership is a recent and international phenomenon. Over recent decades there have been a variety of health service leadership models ranging from general managers, free market models and now we have clinical leadership.

Clinicians are not just doctors but all of us who are involved in healthcare delivery. Nurses, radiographers, dieticians, physiotherapists, speech and language therapist, lab technicians, pharmacists, to name but a few groups, are all in the frame... This could be you! Why not? We all have health sector backgrounds and understand the culture.

Pity the poor clinical leader who is expected to wake up on the first morning of their appointment with management and business skills as well as the clinical skill they trained to have. Being capable in one field does not mean that individuals can automatically do other things. Being a good golfer does not mean we can play tennis. This does not surprise us and yet clinical leaders are put in leadership roles because they are good and capable clinicians, relatively popular reasonable individuals and all round good guys or girls.

The recognition that a different skill set is required and that the individual would benefit from training and understanding of this has been slow to dawn in most health services.

Against this back drop we need pragmatic advice. We need help and we need support. Fundamentally we need that from those who have been there and done it; those who understand the territory; those who can give us knowledge, skills and tools to find our way to our future.

The task is this is not an exact science. A lot is experiential, observational and subjective. It lacks that concrete evidence base we are so wedded to and trained to demand. This is counter intuitive.

This book does not pretend to have the answers to all situations and possibly does not have specific answers to any situations. However it is aimed at opening your eyes and mind to what needs to be considered to allow you to arm yourself with tools and strategies to cope with clinical leadership. It is written in humility from experience good, bad and frankly ugly. Arguably things that have gone wrong are a greater learning experience than the straightforward. Do not seek the optimum organisational organogram or the chapter on finance. They are simply not there! This is not what the book is about. Are clinical leaders heroes or heretics?... Let us park that question and begin our consideration.

CHAPTER 1

Leaders, Managers and Administrators

Consider

- **What is in a name?**
- **Leadership and clinical leadership**
- **Understanding the added value of the 'clinical' element**

Leaders, managers and administrators are all terms in common use in the health service. Probably those using them are aware of what they mean but there is not a common understanding and agreed usage of the terms. Some have a discrete view of the definitions. A leader being a person with a vision who articulates it and aligns colleagues behind it and moves forward. A manager being one who creates a plan to fulfill the strategy and executes it within a performance management structure. The administrator being one who takes specific tasks and elements of the plan forward delegated by the manager and performance managed by them. The manager manages the administrator. The leader on the other hand is a non specific role and might be one of the executive team with responsibility for developing strategy.

I believe these definitions are quite purist and in practical terms are rarely as clear cut or clearly defined or separate from each other.

With no malice of forethought some use the terms interchangeably through ignorance of any difference or a lack of understanding of how the 'system' works. Yet others will use the terms interchangeably and dismissively of clinical colleagues who they believe have 'gone to the dark side' of management.

Thus there is complexity of definition, meaning and understanding not to mention perception.

Let us explore this a little. No health service in the modern age could function without an infra structure of management providing the context for clinical care and service delivery. The domestic and estates function and general housekeeping in relation to hospitals and complex health provision units needs to be managed. Buildings have to be provided and maintained fit for purpose even at a heating and lighting level. They have to be cleaned, modernised and replaced as appropriate. Meals have to be planned, cooked and served. Drugs, medical and surgical supplies have to be sourced, ordered and delivered timeously to ensure constant supply and avoid shortage at times of great and potentially unpredicted demand. Staff have to be employed. Healthcare institutions are multidisciplinary. All staff groups play an important role. Whilst it is perhaps intuitive that a surgeon is necessary to perform operations the whole smooth functioning of an operating theatre depends on the other team members including the anaesthetist, scrub nurse but also theatre nurses and porters who deliver patients from the ward to theatre at the appropriate time and fundamentally the cleaners who have a vital role.

Employment, recruitment and retention require planning, organisation and management. There are robust legal requirements around human resource functions and appropriate training for particular professions and roles. These must be confirmed at times of employment and reaccredidation. In short there are multiple professional roles to be discharged. These are specialised roles and very necessary to the functioning of any healthcare organisation.

It is likely that the need for a robust management infrastructure with finance, human resource, estate and domestic functionality would be agreed by conventional wisdom. The complexity is around the specifics of delivery of healthcare and the need for clinical involvement in that process. This is potentially hugely contentious and multiple constructs of appropriate arrangements are held.

If there is a pure management structure of educated, trained and skilled managers, with general management skills, delivering the functions they require clinical context and information to inform their work. How this is achieved is multifaceted and, at one extreme, there would be an advisory clinical input where advice can be given or be solicited in relation to specific issues with no accountability or responsibility upon the clinician for delivering the service. At the other extreme a pure medical or clinically trained individual would have responsibility and accountability for delivering the service. This is potentially challenging for the clinical manager who is basically operating outside his trained comfort zone of competence. However this model focuses on not just the idealism of pure clinical decision and the best for that patient or group of patients but the pragmatism of affordability and achievability come into the equation as do competing priorities. Medical and clinically trained individuals do not, typically, have the additional training and skill sets to discharge the business aspects of accountability.

There is the added tension of what is the correct decision for an individual patient, what the decision would be in relation to the patient population with a specific disease process or indeed the public at large. This reflects the challenges facing the clinician at the end of the patient's bed who is considering that individual patient and his specific circumstances and what is best for him as opposed to the public health doctor who considers patient populations, percentages and probabilities. The final context is the greater good to the wider public of a particular patient population balanced against other competing possibilities for funding for that disease process and finally in relation to all disease processes, screening and prevention programmes.

The current model of clinical leadership is one of a 'partnership' of an individual with general management skills and training and a clinician. This is deemed to be a useful team to discharge the function. Another model is of a team or executive group providing the wider functions and including clinical input.

Typically administrators and managers are appointed to posts with defined job descriptions around specific responsibilities and accountabilities. They have the authority of their role to discharge their duties.

Clinical leaders may be appointed to roles. In theory they have some status and authority. In practice this is not necessarily the case. Army personnel issue orders and expect obedience and delivery. The police service and typically the ambulance service have this 'command and control' model of management. This is not the ethos of healthcare delivery. Clinical leaders have to negotiate change with colleagues.

Formal appointment of clinical leaders is not the only type of leadership within the health service but rather an element of it. Leadership is a valid concept exhibited in many roles and indeed expected in large numbers of roles in healthcare.

A patient may look to the doctor to lead them through their care. The expectation of knowledge and understanding of the course of the disease and its complications being information the doctor has from experience and learning. He can support and lead the patient through his illness.

Clinicians often have to lead clinical teams and indeed multidisciplinary teams. Both junior staff and other team members, paramedical and allied health professionals, will look to the team leader to adopt that role.

In service change and development there must be leadership. Whilst typically there will be a formal leader appointed others will have to discharge elements of change through discussion, negotiation and adoption of a variety of devices.

In short we may all be called upon to exhibit leadership skills and roles although they are not formally designated as such. In fact they may not be remunerated as such. Some may not recognise they are providing this leadership and indeed might have shied away from applying for a formal leadership role rejecting the perceived burden of the responsibility and accountability.

The focus is probably therefore on the function rather than the form. We should not get too hung up on definitions as it is unlikely we will achieve common agreement and by the way it probably does not matter! It is what we do and how we do it rather than what we call the roles that matters.

Process, structure and function do have their place and it is important to recognise that the above argument in no way denigrates their value. They are the infrastructure of support within which an organisation works. Without them everybody is doing their own thing, in good faith, but typically rather inefficiently. It is inconceivable that any country would function without laws of the land or a highway code. Chaos would ensue however well intentioned individuals were. The default in a large organisation must be known, articulated, documented process which the whole organisation adheres to.

What is at issue here is how to deliver leadership within the context of that framework without enormous bureaucracy and inefficiency. In other words making the system work for you!

Take Home Messages

- **Understand models of leadership**
- **Discover the importance of context, responsibility, expectation, form and function**

CHAPTER 2

So What is Leadership?

Consider

- **The elements of the leadership challenge**

The management books that we all browse through at airports define leadership as

- Having a vision
- Articulating the vision
- Persuading colleagues of the vision
- Moving forward within the vision

Again this is quite purist and idealised. Each step requires careful consideration.

The development of a vision is usually not an educated solitary pursuit but the result of considerable research of possibilities, background and needs of a situation. Typically it is in response to a recognised problem or set of circumstances. It is also the result of distillation of multiple opinions and acknowledgement of down sides as well as advantages and implications of both. In short much consultation precedes it. It is also developed in the context of experience and understanding both of the leader and the situation. Some of us find the vision and horizon scanning aspect of our roles easier than others do. However we do this from our own perspective. The strength is in drawing the views of multiple stakeholders to give a more robust and resilient vision.

In articulating a vision the broad brush sense of where the organisation needs to commit energy and the likely outcome of that is generally the focus rather than how the organisation will get there. Again this may be the product of multiple inputs from staff, patients, referring clinician and budget holding stakeholders.

Alignment behind the vision is easy to say and extremely difficult to deliver particularly if the vision is contentious or perceived to be disadvantageous to any group or individual.

The leader will require involvement and engagement of many to take the vision forward.

In brief, elements of these various skills have been identified as those required of a leader.

Cognitive and analytical skills are necessary to inform a vision together with extrapolatory and predictive skills. An element of foresight informed by knowledge, experience and pragmatism is needed. Good communicative skills are required to broadcast the vision to multiple groups or individuals of different disciplines and different stakeholders with different requirements, aspirations and backgrounds. Collaboration, negotiation, 'boxing and coxing' or juggling ability come into play with vision acceptance. Finally in moving forward, planning and execution skills are required. This sounds a pretty tall order in terms of skill set... a big ask.

Do people with all these skills exist or is this a council of perfection?

There are various models of leadership. Within the medical community the 'great man' has an almost elder statesman status and commands a following. Times change and perhaps this is less prevalent than in the past but it is not entirely extinct. Other have to work harder to achieve an audience for their vision and be persuasive in terms of its adoption. Flexibility of approach is key as is targeting of different audiences. We will explore this further later on.

Clearly we do get things done and many big projects happen so in practical terms leaders do exist. They may not recognise all the steps they go through in completing a project and much may be done intuitively or as a way of working which has been successful for them in the past. However if we are to consider how to go about delivering it is worth giving consideration to the steps and how one can influence each to be more successful more of the time.

Take Home Messages

- **Consider the nature of your leadership challenge**
- **Make leadership work for you**

CHAPTER 3

Leadership Qualities

Consider

- **An understanding of the difference between leadership and authority**
- **Where does the power lie?**

The public perception of leadership is encapsulated in world and political leaders and prime ministers e.g. Margaret Thatcher, Indira Ghandi, Tony Blair and George Bush. It is also embodied in team leaders or captains of high profile sports teams e.g. David Beckham. It is characterised by hereditary aristocracy also e.g. British Queen and the King of Saudi Arabia or Jordan. What do all these individuals have in common if anything?

All have a position of authority and leadership. By designation they have responsibility to deliver.

However leadership may be associated with professional capability and innovation e.g. Marie Curie or indeed peer or public recognition of excellence e.g. Mother Theresa of Calcutta.

I suspect if we asked the man in the street... 'Jo public'... what he required of his leader the answer would be qualities like having a sense of direction, integrity, honesty, hardworking ethic, flexibility, reliability and ability to deliver. He might even suggest ability to deal with high profile and media. Are these so very different from the ones we identified as needed above?

The leadership roles discussed above are appointed, anointed or designated. All have, by their actions found themselves in the roles. Arguably each of these individuals could have conducted themselves in a different way in the past and not have been worthy of the post. Respect has got to be earned it is said and this is a quality one can not have by appointment. Respect is earned by action and example. Typically that is related to a track record around specific actions e.g. achieving on the football field, husbandry of national resource, oratory linked to appropriate national direction or public dignity. The outcome achieved is a following or body of respect which will support and allow an individual to progress his or her agenda unopposed. This may be through competitive preferment for team selection or through the ballot paper in the case of a politician. In the case of royalty the crowds who come to see national celebratory events and expected appearances of royal families or high profile politicians are evidence of this. Media advertisement of Royal appearances guarantee a large crowd of interested observers in most cultures.

We are not all gifted orators but do recognize the advantage of these skills as we watch the persuasive and crowd pulling speeches of Barack Obama. Oratory and vision are a powerful combination and may be perceived as charismatic.

Of course crowds flock to see notoriety also. Historically examples of this are the French Revolution guillotine and public executions. Regrettably where some public disorder is expected this can be a spectator sport for some. However this is not from respect and it is unlikely this would generate the following a leader requires. This just demonstrates that skills can be used for adverse as well as good outcomes.

Leadership qualities will be defined differently by different groups of people. Peers of a leader will have different expectations from those line managed by the same individual. In terms of the clinical context the chief executive will have expectation of his clinical leader to influence colleagues, engender an appetite for change and be in a position to analyse and assimilate information from colleagues in relation to any project. He will want the reality check for any project in terms of clinical appropriateness and credibility and he will want to have clinical prediction of down sides as well as advantage. In short he will want to work in partnership with the clinical leader. The clinician should bring the clinical risk profile of change to the chief executive and give an understanding of impacts and unplanned and unintended consequences of actions.

Peers will want an open approach with consideration and respect for their points of view and their agenda with collaborative working being the preferred outcome and modus operandi.

Those line managed by the leader will want their jobs considered in relation to any change in the organisation. They will want their 'voice heard' in terms of aspirations. They will also want to be kept informed and have awareness of what is planned particularly if it has implications for them. They will want to be looked after and their interest looked out for.

Again are we setting clinical leaders up for failure having all these expectations of them?

The concept of managing expectations comes into play. The unrealistic hope or expectation should be addressed early.

The clinical leader needs to consider what he regards his role as being.

Take Home Messages

- **Respect must be earned**
- **Lead by example**
- **Understand and manage expectations**

CHAPTER 4

The Leadership Role

Consider

- **Role definition versus doing the job**
- **Self awareness**
- **Awareness of others**
- **Interface awareness**
- **Understanding matched and mismatched priorities**

The leadership role may be formally identified in a job description and have been discussed through an interview and recruitment process. Some leadership posts are still annointments and therefore little formal agreed expectation is documented. This is not good news. Or rather there is good news and bad news on this realistically. Where there is no written expectation the clinical leader is apparently free to have his own construct of the role and expectation of him. This is fine in a tightly managed team where expectation may be verbally explicit and there are checks and balances. However where the clinical leader sets off with his own role profile and that is not consonant with his line manager problems may arise.

It is always a good idea to discuss the role profile. Even if a job description has been available. The actual discharge of the duties are best to have detailed attention. This is useful at the time of applying for the post although that is an information gathering exercise to inform the decision to apply. After appointment it is essential to have a shared understanding of the role in terms of specific tasks, focus, approach and mechanisms of communication. Early and frequent meetings with the chief executive or line manager are a really good idea. The building up of a working relationship is essential. Working relationships are founded on self awareness, understanding of the approach of others and awareness of their needs in order that when there are pressures, challenging tasks and difficult situations are being dealt with each can support the other and individual strengths can be played to.

During the course of a clinical leader's career constant search for feedback, reflection and checking of understanding in relation to requirement upon him and his approach will pay dividends.

Within any framework of job description and discussion about the role profile the clinical leader still has to consider how he will 'do the job'. In doing this he needs to consider

- Values and beliefs
- Priorities

- Expectation and aspiration of the role
- Stakeholders
- Stakeholder expectation
- Communication strategy
- Exit strategy

Values and Beliefs

We are all hardwired with our own code of conduct. Our principles, how we behave and how we interact with others both in a work and general life setting. This reflects how we have been brought up, our education, background, religious and moral beliefs and our experience of life. It is said you can not change an individual's value systems. It is important therefore to understand these and to respect one's own values and at the same time recognise that others may have a different set of values to which they are wedded. Any challenge to these may be difficult for them and result in a perception of conflict. This does not mean being overt in finding out religious beliefs or specific political views but it does mean considering that your own approach may not be shared by others and their right to hold a different perspective is valid and should be respected. Individuals may hold views for obvious and predictable reasons or for reasons that are not overt in some cases or frankly obscure in others. For instance if we have had an experience of sudden death of a family member at an early age this may influence our thinking. We might or might not feel able to share this information and indeed we might not even see the connection in relation to how that has influenced our thinking in any particular situation.

Priorities

Whilst respect of other's views seems an implicit strength and a sensible approach this may be quite challenging in terms of delivering on organisational priorities. The best metaphor I have heard in relation to this is the baby in the back seat.

If one is driving along with a baby strapped into a car seat in the back of the car and the baby chokes it seems entirely appropriate, at the next set of traffic lights to stop, get out of the car and dive into the back seat to help the baby. This course of action will not seem so appropriate to the person driving the car behind. Depending on the context of their day they may exclaim and shake their head if they are having a relaxed day and are in no hurry. However if they are late for a dental appointment which they have waited 6 weeks for they may have an 'emotional response'. The emotional response is one we have less control over and exhibits itself as fight or flight. In this circumstance standing on the horn for a long and continuous period might ensue as a rather aggressive gesture or they too may get out of the car to remonstrate. I think you will get the picture.

We all have different priorities. We must never assume the priorities of others match our own. It is also useful to remember that priorities change with time and with issue. Again no assumptions should be made but constant checking of understanding through open questions and free communication confirm views. Asking always reveals more information than telling. Seek first to understand the views of others and their position. In understanding their views their concerns will become apparent and can be addressed.

Expectation and Aspiration of the Role

Specifics may be covered in the job description and we have considered that various individuals and groups will have different expectations and aspirations in relation to the role. The chief executive will want delivery and a sympathetic ear to his agenda with suggestions on how to take this forward appropriately with the clinical community. Peers and those being line managed will have a different expectation. What of the clinical leader himself? What is his expectation of the role? Nobody comes to work to do a bad job it is said. He will want to deliver an appropriate service in relation to his construct of the needs of the situation.

We are all heroes in our own minds and we all act appropriately in relation to our own values and priorities. However there is the need to understand one's own expectations and those of others and to identify conflicts of views or aspiration. Basically it is very difficult to please all of the people all of the time including ourselves. It is not sensible to be aiming for the popular approach. There is a job to be done. Usually it is good to understand and manage differences and steer the appropriate course managing adverse impacts through acknowledgement through foresight.

Stakeholders

In order to have a balanced and balancing overview of views on any particular issue an understanding of who the stakeholders are is required. Performance of the leadership role is an example of where there will be stakeholders. Typically these may be

- Chief executive of healthcare institution
- Other executives of healthcare institution e.g. Director of Finance
- Peers e.g. nurse and other clinical leads
- Those who are being line managed e.g. those with operational responsibility to deliver the service
- Clinical governance leads/ Quality assurance leads
- Patients
- The public
- The Funding authority
- Higher Education Institutions
- The Government

This list is not exhaustive but to give a feel for the extent of ramification of consideration both of inputs and outputs of leader's actions. All the above list will have views on issues. These may be personally expressed, implicit or part of a specific documented policy or government directive. A listening brief of awareness is helpful. All will not come into play on all occasions. For complex issues it is sometimes worth actually jotting down a list of stakeholders.

Stakeholder Expectation

The next step is to consider what perspective each stakeholder or group will have in relation to any specific issue. Some of this will be predictable and certain. Some will be speculative. All is useful information. There are various levels of 'need' and 'want' around this. Some stakeholders will have an absolute right to have a view and influence an issue by dint of post, account-abilities and responsibility. Others on the other hand may want to know as a matter of information, courtesy or frank curiosity. Consideration of impacts of a course of action on stakeholders and stakeholder groups is useful. This can be both positive impact which may be welcome or adverse impacts which are best acknowledged and managed. Ignoring or minimising indi-vidual adverse impact is likely to be a recipe for disaster and likely to come back and 'bite you'.

Communication Strategy

Once stakeholders and their needs and wants are considered a communication strategy can be established. This sounds immensely formal but in fact consideration as to who needs to know for different purposes and who wants to know for infor-mation will tease out the following

- Those responsible for developing the vision
- Those who need to understand the vision in order to plan steps towards it
- Those who need to understand the steps to execute the plan
- Those who need to be aware it is happening as a matter of cour-tesy or anticipation of unexpected consequences good and bad

Again the example of how the clinical leadership role is performed is relevant to this generic approach which can be used issue by issue.

There is also a sequence of communication thereafter. The vision development is an early phase. Planning, execution and awareness follow later. As a general rule the phases are not discrete but overlap and some individuals may be involved at more than one phase. Others may only be involved in one. By anticipating the needs of each the communication strategy is more likely to be robust. Usually when individuals and groups are aware of an issue and have a platform or opportunity to have their views of potential impacts heard and acknowledged this minimises difficulty later in terms of acceptance. This is sometimes described as 'getting over the grief reaction'.

Exit Strategy

Let us revert to the clinical leadership role. In taking on such a role the skills and competencies are different from the medical, nursing or allied health professional role in which the leader has skill, education and accredited competencies. The formal education and examination in relation to the professional competence will have lead to a qualification. At this point in time clinical leadership is not formally accredited and there is no requirement to have any specific training prior to embarking on the role. Increasingly the skills and competencies required are being acknowledged and training packages are being put in place in the form of management courses and leadership courses. It is now common place for medical consultants in the UK, for instance, to have attended a management course before embarking on their consultant career. More senior consultants and those who may be in the frame in terms of clinical leadership may not have had that opportunity. Enlightened organisations facilitate this and consider psychometrics, mentoring and coaching as elements of good practice to support the clinical leader in taking on the role. Many organisations have well developed Organisational Development Departments who can support this. Peer support and networking is increasingly having a role. The legitimacy of this activity has been an issue in terms of time allocation and funding where travel has been necessary. With time this valid support is being acknowledged.

There is still a cohort of frontier clinical leaders who shun psychometrics, self awareness and self reflection as a necessary part of understanding themselves and their role. It is a sort of 'real men do not eat quiche' syndrome or macho culture and seen as something of a weakness to require this support. They would rather shoulder all responsibility and 'deal with it all' in their own way. The lack of recognition of the other valid perceptions of situations and lack of awareness of other methods of 'dealing with' issues is a substantial weakness of their approach.

It is commonplace for clinical leaders to be appointed through due recruitment and selection processes of increasing rigour but with no previous experience. Inevitably the basis for individuals applying for the post varies. Typically some of the following apply:

- Wanting to make a difference
- Wanting to progress a particular service or project
- Wanting new skills
- Wanting a change of direction in career

- Peer pressure
- Their individual turn

The best case scenario is the individual wants to take on the role rather than finding, it is, in the eyes of their colleagues, their turn. Under these circumstances individuals may put themselves forward with 'heart sink' feelings.

Respected colleagues who are seen as even handed, fair and reasonable with some ability to influence and some popularity may find themselves promoted by colleagues for such roles. They are persuaded into the role. Caution should be exercised under these circumstances as relationships with peers change when one is in a leadership role. Difficult decisions have to be made for legitimate reasons and colleagues may feel let down if their particular point of view is not supported or progressed as they feel appropriate. They may not have access or inclination to access all information which informed a decision. There is a difference between representing colleagues and line managing or leading them. This may be considered as the difference between being the trade union representative and the manager of the colleagues.

Individuals taking Leadership roles can be wounded by the change in attitude to them by peers and find the new relationship isolating. Peers may have difficulty separating challenging issues from the personality of the leader as an individual. 'Mud sticks' to the leader in relation to issues he is progressing. Even long standing friendships can come under pressure. Support networks are vital. Some find this easy to establish. Others never make this jump. Active consideration of this is useful in terms of natural allies of the role.

Where the motivation for taking the role on has been aligned to a specific project or service development the challenge will be to grasp the full agenda and have enthusiasm and energy to devote to the whole role rather than the particular interest. Some are more successful than others. The case of members of a parliament or government being appointed in relation to a 'hot' political item in a single constituency is probably a useful parallel. Their interest being around a local hospital closure for instance. These individuals rarely go on to have a second term in office.

Where the role is being undertaken with intention of developing new skills and exploring a new career direction enthusiasm is often optimum. The individual approaches the new role with a sense of freshness, application and enthusiasm. They are exploring whether this is something they have any aptitude for. Clinical leadership is something of a Pandora's Box. Until it is opened the contents are not apparent. Until one is in the role and exploring it one doesn't really know what is involved and if it is 'for you'. Outside perception of roles can be quite skewed in their impression and assumption of what is involved. The reality may be quite different.

Under all circumstances it is as well to consider,on taking on a clinical leadership role, what next steps will be. It may be that the role suits well. It is a new set of challenges which the individual enjoys and the different contact with clinical colleagues and a fresh range of colleagues with other skills e.g. finance, human resources and management skills is stimulating. In which case progress and further involvement will be the way forward. This could be to more senior clinical leadership either within the single organisation or regionally or nationally;

the latter being strategic where the local involvement may be more operational. Strategic clinical leaders are always most valued when they have experience of operational management and therefore the credibility of having 'been there' and really understanding the pressures.

However it may be the case that the clinical leader finds the new challenges and the altered relationship with colleagues destructive and something he does not want to continue with. It is as well to anticipate that a range of possibilities exist on embarking on the leadership adventure and ensure that there is either a way back to full time in the clinical area or other acceptable situation. If boats are burned then options are limited. Nobody sets off to do a bad job. However some tasks and roles suit better than others in terms of role. This is not entirely predictable. A secondment rather than complete move to the new role has some attraction as it allows this return with dignity if leadership turns out not to be your thing. A sense of limited trial is better than a climb down and sense of failure of permanent appointment.

Some undertake leadership roles at the end of their career. The exit strategy is retirement. However it should not be assumed just because one is senior and experienced that leadership will come naturally or that it will be something you can do to effect or enjoy.

Go into leadership roles with your eyes open. Consider what the risks are to you in relation to your career. It is also worth considering that the organisation may not find your style or ability suitable. If you can, try to consider the organisational risk of you doing the role and what the organisation wants from you in relation to it.

Explicit discussion around exit strategy at the time of appointment is a good idea. Typically leadership roles have a fixed duration but this is frequently extended. Some, however, have no fixed term. A drifting situation with unmatched expectations is unhelpful all round.

Theoretically this all sounds fine and possibly even intuitive. The context can add complexity. Health Services are subject to continuous public, media and government scrutiny. This reflects the large sums of money involved in delivery and the general population interest. In such large and unwieldy organisations the temptation for governments to reorganise the structure and mechanisms of delivery are almost irresistible where these are nationalised services. The result being there is a rapid turn over of senior executives and chief executives. It is said the average life of chief executives in UK NHS organisations is between 2 and 3 years. Clinicians will, however, be around organisations for many years. Medical consultants can be in post for 30 years for instance.

The danger for a clinical leadership role is that the post may be reorganised out of the organisation. Or that 'the face' of the clinical leader does not fit with the new administration. The adage that 'if we always do what we have always done we will always get what we always had' comes into play. Where there is a reorganisation the chief executive will be required to make a change which will involve doing things differently. However hard one has worked or aligned one's self to the organisational agenda one may be seen as 'yesterday's man' and marginalised by the new chief executive who wants new and different blood for different outcomes. Recognition of this may be helpful in terms of placing one's self for involvement in the new regime.

However it may be completely beyond individual capability to influence this. This is dispiriting and potentially demotivating. There is no easy answer. Recognition that this may be absolutely nothing to do with individual performance but rather alliance with previous administration's agenda is vital in terms of individual resilience.

The exit strategy under these circumstances can feel quite uncomfortable and thrust upon us. We can jump or be pushed. We can resist and try to cling to the past values and agenda. The latter is unlikely to be fruitful and indeed can be destructive in terms of perception of others. The ability to recognise the reality of the situation is a strong indicator of ability to continue and reinvent one's self to be useful to the organisation by applying one's strengths in a different way or adapting the previous agenda to organisational advantage. The organisation will be in turmoil however well contained. Recognising this and the fact that under these circumstances individuals and their roles and futures will not be the priority of the executive team is valuable insight. This is not easy territory when one may feel vulnerable and undervalued.

It is said that if one is in control then it limits stress. Stress is generated by lack of ability to influence the future or one's place in it. Accordingly analyse the situation and develop a plan. The facets of this plan should include

- Acknowledgement of the future direction of the organisation (the vision)
- Work to date which can be built on
- Information which is required
- Plan of actions and steps needed to fulfil the new vision

- What roles and actions are needed to deliver
- What you can offer personally

This will require analysis of the situation from your own perspective but also checking understanding with other stakeholders. In considering next steps, impacts and unintended consequences for groups and individuals can be checked with other stakeholders and colleagues. This should not be an magnum opus but astute rapid piece of work which should be shared with the line management team and chief executive early. This shows willingness to let go of the past and also an aptitude to do so. We all have 'baggage'. This can be regarded as experience and a positive thing or negative thinking which is unhelpful. In terms of influencing the future we need to accentuate the positive even if the coming to terms with that is done behind closed doors at the end of the day in terms of personal impact.

Clearly carving out a place for one's self is the objective. If you can not see yourself in the future it is difficult to persuade an executive team of your role.

It is always useful to be able to discuss this with a disinterested peer. By that I mean one who is not in competition with you for future roles. Possibly a colleague from another organisation, discipline or division can give that objectivity and can help you to challenge your own thinking. This is mentoring really. A mentor allows you to explore your own thinking and come to your own conclusions by asking questions and reflecting back thinking. A coach on the other hand gives us tools and techniques to try in a variety of circumstances. There are rafts of methodologies and as we are all different. What works for one does not necessarily work for another. This is worth bearing in mind. Reject no thought until you have considered and tested it in your own situation.

Emotional intelligence is a term used to describe resilience founded on one's own feelings and emotions and those of others. It is the ability, to identify, assess and manage our own emotions, those of other individuals and groups. It can be traced back to instincts and Darwin's thinking which identified the importance of the ability to adapt to survive. This has an emotional element. Understanding emotions allows the possibility of managing them to advantage through anticipation and acknowledgement. Various models exist but basically are self awareness, self management, social awareness and relationship management all of which are amenable to training and learned capability enhancement. These are not innate talents. This is scratching at the surface of a large body or work which has become a compelling observational literature.

Take Home Messages

- **First know thy self**
- **Seek first to understand: active listening**
- **Respect others and their views**
- **Pragmatism in the face of adversity**

CHAPTER 5

Perception

Consider

- **Understanding perception**
- **Refining understanding**
- **Achieving productive discussion**

Individual Perception

It is easy to assume that our thinking on a matter is shared thinking and the conclusions we draw from sets of information will be those of others. Why should this be the case at work when it is not the case in general life? We do not all like the same television programmes. We do not all like sport, the same sort of music, the same cars or types of holiday. Yet we do all have access to the same advertising, television listings and holiday brochures. We are all different. Is this completely unpredictable? How does one approach a project or issue where there may be different view points? Can they be flushed out, understood and a mutually agreeable action decided. Is there a way of explaining the issue to best advantage?

Seek first to understand the adage goes. Yes it will be important to understand the perception of others. If we go back to the principles we laid out an exercise can be undertaken in relation to a specific project or desired course of action e.g. new service or different method of providing a service e.g. role enhancement. The following steps are worth considering

- Consider who the stakeholders are
- Consider what the advantage of the change will be to them
- Consider adverse impacts
- Consider unintended consequences
- Consider their anxieties
- Explore information necessary to understand change impact.

This can be done as a solitary exercise and homework prior to embarking on any consultation about a change in service. It will be personal information to inform approach. It can also be a more formal consideration involving the team allocated to take the change forward. It therefore functions at different levels.

A good rule of thumb is to be in listening mode. Actively listen to what people are saying and what they are not saying or acknowledging. It is good to have 'all the blood out on the carpet' and be in a position to deal with anxieties. Not everybody is comfortable with stating their concerns if they believe them to be selfish or 'not politically correct' for instance. For example antisocial hours in an extended day might be very difficult for a staff group to take on but may be undeniably better for the patient in terms of access to the service. This is an extreme example to make the point. This issue would have contractural consequences and would be subject to great scrutiny in reality and would involve trade unions as legitimate stakeholders.

Time spent understanding personal concerns, service agendas, personal aspirations and group thinking is not time wasted.

Appreciative Inquiry is a device to do this. The clinical leader or facilitator of the discussion asks a question and allow the team member to express a view. The facilitator then reflects the information back positively in his own words encouraging further information and views. 'Let me see I have understood how you see this…', 'That is a good point can you enlarge on it for me…' Again this is subject of reflection etc. The outcome is the team member feels they have had a good hearing. No judgment has been made but rather exploration of thinking and concerns for the future. This is likely to be achievable without fracturing any relationships as no contrary view is introduced. By marrying up the views of multiple team members from multiple disciplines then a more holistic view of perceptions can be arrived at.

Never assume one's own view of the world is shared. We all have different personality profiles. There are many methods of psychometric testing which give us different ways of understanding the range. One of the best known and frequently used methods is the Myers-Briggs Type Indicator.* This is often used as a team or group rather than in isolation. It is performed by those with formal training as feedback and interpretation is very

---

*Gifts Differing; Understanding Personality Type, Ishbel Briggs Myers with Peter B Meyers (1980) Consulting Psychologists Press, Inc.

important. This is fed back as information and reflection of style and preference. There is no judgment involved.

Initially teams are asked which hand they choose to write with. They are then encouraged to take a pencil and write their name with the other hand. Individuals are able to do that usually but it is not the preferred way of writing. This is not their preferred style. The understanding is the Myers-Briggs Indicator is about personality preferences. Nothing is right or wrong. There is a range. One adopts certain styles for preference but one can adopt others under certain circumstances. This is about preferences. Awareness of one's preferences and those of one's colleagues can influence approach and style of communication which will achieve desired outcomes. The main part of the indicator tool is a questionnaire based on choices. This is not the place to lay out the styles in detail suffice it to say there are 16 recognised styles. There is a summary word which will be how the world sees each style in its purest form

- Inspector
- Protector
- Counselor
- Mastermind
- Crafter
- Composer
- Healer
- Architect
- Promoter
- Performer
- Champion
- Inventor

- Supervisor
- Provider
- Teacher
- Field Marshal

Of course this is a range of style preferences and we adopt different styles as well as our preferred one so this is not a pure art or science. Under certain circumstances we all behave differently and may recognize ourselves in several of the descriptive words in different situations. For instance one's preferred style may be around the 'inspector' preference with deeply analytical approach to the world. When given complex task to complete this style is very useful. However having done the analysis delivery of a plan of action and outcomes will be necessary and the preferred style may need to be flexed to one or more of the other styles. Individuals will do that as a matter of course but may recognise that they prefer doing the analysis to the actual planning or delivery function.

You may wish to explore this in detail. You can do this by approaching the Organisational Development Team in your own organisation or simply by going on the internet which has shoals of information about Myers-Briggs but also many other psychometric tests which can be applied. Awareness of the different styles is the issue here.

If we understand our own style it is, in many instances, predictable how we will behave or react in certain circumstances. We may think we know this already. Styles dictate if we derive our information about the outside world from intuition or rely on facts; if we are interested in people impacts or task outcomes; if we like to consider possibilities or come to a rapid outcome. Our focus will be different. The context is whether we derive our energy from action and in the outside world or if we internalise or reflect. The topic is endlessly fascinating and there is much literature on it. Do read more.

Intellectually there is a satisfaction in pure models but life is not like that. The Myers-Briggs Indicator also gives us a feel as to how 'extreme' our preference is. Again no judgment here but rather how we would compare with the population generally. It is useful to know that some colleagues will do all their thinking out loud and develop their responses 'on the hoof' in conversation exploring thoughts and taking new information in from themselves and others as they go. Other colleagues will have done the analysis internally and when they speak will have completed their thinking and present the outcome of that.

At the interface of these two extreme cases perceptions will be interesting if neither colleague understands how the other develops their thinking. The first colleague will seem to be inconclusive and lacking out come focus to the second colleague whilst the second colleague will seem rigid and unbending to the first.

First know thy self it is said. This makes a lot of sense. Understanding one's own style allows comparison with others. We tend to know our colleagues quite well and some of their responses to situations will be predictable just from custom and practice. We may even have a judgment associated with how they will react. 'He will be inflexible' or 'She will never make up her mind'. The strength of this approach is awareness of the style preference will allow us to have a more productive discussion with them on their terms. Not to diminish our own needs but to have the discussion in such a way as it feels a positive experience around the facts and needs of the issue rather than a clash of styles.

Knowledge is power.

The added value of this is if we know our team members and consider their style preferences we can then craft a discussion in such a way to satisfy their needs and wants in terms of allowing thinking to develop as well as acknowledge that some thinking has been developed already. Active acknowledgement of different approaches and styles is helpful 'You will have something interesting to contribute to this...what have you been thinking?' 'Where are you in your thinking on this one?...'

Take Home Messages

- **Perception is all**
- **Never assume**
- **Seek first to understand**
- **Non judgmental exploration**

CHAPTER 6

Team Working

Consider

- **'Group think concept'**
- **Team strengths**
- **Team balance**

Teams are complex beasts. Generally we do not have the opportunity to pick our team but are presented with at least part of it. We may even inherit it from a previous clinical leader. This may feel uncomfortable and some of the team members may not have been our intuitive choice of people to work with. PLU... people like us. Life is sometimes at its most comfortable if we have like minded people around us. We all then consider problems in the same way. We are likely to come to the same conclusions and there is little disharmony. In other words we have 'group think'. Whilst this may feel like a comfort zone it is an enormous missed opportunity.

Another way of analysing interactions is to look at the skills of individuals in an ideal team and consider if the team you have has the full range. There are a number of tools to do this which are questionnaire based. The Belbin Team* Role is probably amongst the best known of this and certainly one in common usage. The roles are

- Plant
- Resource Investigator
- Coordinator
- Shaper
- Monitor Evaluator
- Team Worker
- Implementer
- Completer Finisher
- Specialist

Again this is not the place to go into the detail of this methodology. You can explore the literature or even the internet which is such a rich source of information without significant cost. The idea is to give insight into the thinking and possibilities around it.

Each member of a team will exhibit some of these strengths. Some will excel in one and have a less strong capability in others. Team balance is very important. Where possible it is good to consider all the elements of a team and ensure that holistically the team has the full range of skills. As an example if a team is strong on visionary thinking and resource investigators

---

*Belbin M (1981) Management Teams, London, Heinemann but also consider visiting the website on www.belbin.com.

but has no team workers or completer finishers agreeing and delivering outcomes will be very challenging...and neither will there be any team sign up to doing so.

To each and every action there is an opposite reaction. This is a principle in physics but translates for our purpose. For every team role style there is an interpretation. This may be useful and positive or perceived as unhelpful and in a negative way. Again this is worth recognising. The resource investigator may be extrovert, enthusiastic and a great communicator. He explores opportunities and develops good personal contacts. However his weakness is over optimism and a tendency to lose interest after the initial enthusiasm. The coordinator is mature, confident and a great chairperson with clear goals, decision making and delegation skills. However they may be seen as manipulative, controlling and as off loading personal work.

In appointing a team it is good to consider the profile of the team roles within the team already and recruit to gaps. The trap that we must avoid is appointing 'in one's own image' i.e. the like minded with the matching skill set. This might make for cosy committee meetings but will be unhelpful in progressing the agenda and the organisation.

As a principle it is a different matter choosing friends and life partners from choosing colleagues and team members for work. It seems strange to articulate this but it may be something we have to give more active consideration to!

Typically we do not have the luxury of appointing a team from scratch but rather augmenting the one we have. Open discussion and acknowledgement of team strengths and areas for development are helpful in considering additional team members and constructing the job description and job advertisement. The challenge is to marry this up with the professional skills individuals bring to a team e.g. finance or specific clinical input.

We all bring something to the party. Acknowledgement of this is important. Each contribution should be sought and each should be valued. Where there is a dominant force in a committee or team who overtly or covertly drowns out others contributions through the strength of their input this is not strength but a weakness in taking forward a balanced outcome. Those railroaded or run rough shod over are much less likely to be on board for change. If, however, individual thinking, perceptions and views have been explored whatever the final result of team or committee is the group is more likely to be behind the decision. They will feel they have been part of the discussion, part of the decision and can be part of the way forward.

A very important aspect of team working is mutual respect. Respect has got to be earned and does not come with the appointment as authority does. Respect is developed by action, by behaviour and usually over time. In many ways respect is a spectator driven quality. It is in the eyes of the beholder. It is how we are regarded not how we want to be regarded. We can not make people respect us even if we want to. We can, however, influence this through our integrity and actions. It is about how we treat each other, our peers, those we line manage and those who line manage us. It is about how we apply our values.

If we are overt, consistent, honest and fair an interpretation is put on this. If we are, on the other hand, covert, underhand and inconsistent in our approach those around us form a view and are cautious in their dealings with us. Such actions may achieve a once off objective but in terms of building up a long term relationship within a team or committee we are storing up trouble and lack of cooperation for ourselves. We all like people who like us and typically respect those who respect us. Trust is built on respect. In a team if all contributions are valued and respected this is a good foundation for trust. Where there is mutual respect and trust in a team, work can be shared and the amount of duplication of effort is minimised. Each trusts the other to deliver appropriately to the benefit of the team.

Team working is not about the battle it is about the campaign. It is the long term relationship not the 'one off' agenda item, project or decision.

Teams have a common focus by dint of their existence. Individual team members will have special responsibilities in terms of knowledge and delivery but the effort is a holistic team one. Accordingly when the team is working on a project the differing perceptions, knowledge and skills brought to bear are valid and necessary. This allows the team full discussion and appropriate informed decision making. This is not to say the team will hold all the cards and knowledge or indeed have all the skills but they are likely to 'know a man' who does have any missing bit of the information jig saw and solicit that information to inform decision making.

In exploring thinking challenge is valid to elicit understanding of different perception. We can all be sensitive about challenge. The way this is done is important. If one feels passionately about a particular development stating a point of view in an empassioned way may feel rather overbearing to those listening who may hold a different perception. This may be accentuated if one's style is to do thinking out loud and 'on the hoof' whilst presenting a case...and further still if the rest of the team are more introspective reflectors developing their thinking in a quieter more internalised way. Beware of loosing the respect of your colleagues and the strength or your argument points through approach. Consider

- Measured approach
- Acknowledging different perceptions
- Laying out of risk profiles
- Balanced argument
- Conclusions.

On the other hand some colleagues may find challenge destructive and may withdraw from discussion in the face of an empassionate presentation of counter argument. Whilst the protagonist may feel they have won their case that might or might not be true. The subdued colleague may still have a perception that needs explored. This can come 'back to bite' later as they nurse their point of view. They have not had full scope to express it or wrestle the issue to the ground through full team discussion.

Clinical leaders do hold views passionately. Particularly patient relate issues of safety and quality which goes to the very heart of what they do. There is nothing wrong in this; quite the reverse. However presentation of views is all and allowing full discussion and different views air time is an important part of the role.

Take Home Messages

- **Value the differences**
- **Acknowledge different inputs**
- **Mutual respect and trust**
- **Long term relationships**

CHAPTER 7

Team Building

Consider

- **Adding value**
- **Nurturing the team**

Whether we construct our own team or inherit a full team or part of one nurturing and developing the team is a responsibility the clinical leader should take seriously. As you sew so shall you reap. What is put into team building pays rich rewards. When the pressure is on and the situation a team is facing is difficult team spirit and ability to pull together is important. Supporting each other through complex situations is a real team strength. This does not just happen.

Team building needs sewing, watering and nurturing in gardening terms. The team should sink or swim together. We have discussed both individual style profiles and we have discussed team role profiles. Both these form useful information upon which to build team spirit. In a new team this might be too big a step for individuals who do not know each other and how have not yet 'worked' each other out or the appropriate respect and trust profiles. The team needs to get to know each other. Inevitably this is easier in a social or quasi social setting. This can be done through formal team building exercises with outside management consultants (potentially at great cost!) or with the more cheap and cheerful team night out to a local restaurant. We have sometimes combined a leveler of ten pin bowling or a departmental walk with a meal after. The ice skating event produced a completely unsuspected star as did the clay pigeon shooting event. Do not get the impression that it is all pleasure and no work at my institution — far from it. These have been annual events over many years. The bonding and multidisciplinary team spirit generated is a real pleasure to experience and real friendships have emerged.

Initiation of these events may be a bit challenging. Not everybody is a party animal and wants to socialise with work colleagues. Whilst not advocating a command performance in terms of attendance a recognition of the need for generating enthusiastic participation is worth considering.

The nurturing aspect is a commitment to this being a way of working and not just a one off event. It is a mind set. We should all 'look after' other team members and support them and their agendas. This generates support for ourselves in return and can extend beyond the boundaries of our hospitals, surgeries and healthcare institutions. We are not usually in competition with team members so collaboration is a healthy approach.

Where team relationships have been difficult or where there is regular strife then the leader does have a role in recognising this and considering action. Exploration of difference and recognition of each contribution being valid is a good starting point. Awareness of the richness of different perspectives and respecting individual rights to hold these is important. The aim is collective praise for the team.

Teams, in many respects have an organisational life of their own. It is said they go through four phases to development

- Forming
- Storming
- Norming
- Performing

Leadership is important at each phase and necessary to support the group through the highs of initial enthusiasm of getting together and potential lows of differing points of view which may seem negative and challenging before reaching an understanding of each other's strengths and team contribution, eventually developing ways of working to add value to the organisation.

Some 'teams' are a set piece in terms of membership. The membership may be made up of a number of appointed roles e.g. the Board of a Health Care Institution may have a Chief Executive, Director of Finance, Medical and Nurse Director to name but a few. Each of these will have a specific role in terms of their job description and expectations upon them. Both the Medical and Nurse Director will have responsibilities around ensuring clinical governance and patient safety for the organisation together with other corporate responsibilities. The particular added value they bring is the understanding of the cultural context, clinical implications and clinical risk profile of Board decisions. Their contribution may sometimes be quite difficult to reconcile with that of the Director of Finance but each party brings a necessary piece of the jigsaw of the full view. The Board strength is to seek and value all contributions in arriving at appropriate decisions.

Take Home Messages

- **Recognise different perspectives**
- **Seek and value different perspectives**
- **Mutual support**

CHAPTER 8

Team Leader

Consider

- **Bad behaviour and ground rules**
- **Team and team leader responsibilities**

The team leader has a very important role in setting the course of the team but also the behaviours and ways of working. Formal consideration of these important practices early in the life of a team or at any stage is worth considering. Team 'bad behaviour' is unhelpful as a long term way of working and is destructive to the reputation of the team. Ground rules might include

- Each team member has a right to express their view
- All views are valid
- All views are respected
- All views are valued

- After full discussion the team forms a view which the team will agree
- The view will be promoted and supported outside the team setting

If the team is having a bad time wrestling with a difficult issue it is good if they can share and discuss that internally with other team members not 'dump' or whine about the unresolved issue elsewhere. This enhances the perception of team integrity and cohesiveness. Car park post mortems trying to overturn team decision help nobody.

The leader often has the accountability and responsibility for team actions particularly if he has been formally appointed to the role. However it is important that he does not hold all the information and all the power of the committee or team. He needs to be able to delegate with authority and confidence. This generates trust in the team and also builds capacity for extending skills and sharing the load. Delegation is a skill like any other. Clear direction of the expected outcome and sometimes method of getting there with timescale are important. It is also vital that any interim follow up by him is defined at the outset. He must not be seen to interfere or take the task back or run a parallel project. He must not pick at it like a scab in short. If there are issues about the ability of the person to whom the task is delegated then clear lines of performance management should be laid out at the start and followed.

When a clinical leader moves on the team should not fall apart. One of the facets of leadership is succession planning for the team and building capacity and resilience. Many situations arise where leaders move on (sometimes to greater things and sometimes not!) at short notice so this is particularly worth considering.

The team and leadership mind set is important. Value the difference. It is a strength. Welcome challenge! It is information about a different perception that we may not have considered. There is a school of thought that there are some perceptions that are hidden to us.

It is said we should value complaints. They are free feedback in relation to the service we provide. Again we may feel this as challenge and take this personally. We feel blamed and we feel guilty. A consideration of the approach and mindset in relationship to this is worth considering.

Take Home Messages

- **Creating team and team leader mind sets**
- **Valuing the difference as a positive move**
- **Team resilience**

CHAPTER 9

Complaints and Feedback

Consider

- **The place of feedback**
- **'No blame culture'**
- **Professional handling**

Most complaints, incidents and occurrences are not down to a personal failure but rather system errors which are multifactorial. It is easy to look at the very specific issue the complaint has raised and jump to a conclusion about who was responsible, what they did wrong and blame them. This has translated to suspensions and disciplining in the past. We do have a more enlightened perception of the complaints function and indeed marry it up with various forms of occurrence and near miss reporting systems. All these give us information about how well a team and organisation are functioning. By collecting this information we are able to identify trends and transferable lessons which the team and organisation can use as information to help develop its future mode of working.

There are formal approaches to investigating complaints and occurrences and probably Root Cause Analysis as advocated by the Institute of Healthcare Improvement* is one of the best known. This methodology allows full and open exploration of the circumstances of the occurrence and contributory factors. The aim being to acknowledge what has happened, to apologise where appropriate and develop a factual explanation through accounts of events from the involved colleagues. Then analyse what the route causes were. Typically these are multifactorial

- Patient Factors
- Individual Factors
- Task Factors
- Communication Factors
- Team and Social Factors
- Education and Training Factors
- Equipment and Resource Factors
- Working Condition Factors
- Organisational and Strategic Factors

The approach is structured and widely known in an organisation using the methodology. This is more comfortable for those

---

*www.ihi.org. This is a very valuable web site and a route to access to a lot of improvement methodology and tools for individuals and teams to consider. These have been developed by the Institute of Healthcare Improvement and many examples of their application are available together with practical advice.

involved who then have confidence that this is not a random process.

The analysis involves identification of contributory factors and eventually the root causes. This allows a formal report and action plan when the incident is of sufficient seriousness to merit this.

Whilst individual occurrences and near misses are important the trends and transferable lessons are vital to an organisation in developing its governance structure. The clinical leader has a role in interpreting the trends and ensuring the transferable lessons are acted upon and communicated appropriately.

The 'no blame culture' is talked about glibly. Whilst an open minded approach to occurrences and complaints is necessary and circumstances will frequently reveal multifactorial root causes individuals may have acted inappropriately. The organisation requires to have a 'just culture' so that individuals recognise they will be treated fairly. This does not mean individuals will be summararily dismissed but rather consideration be given to retraining and standard setting together with review of general departmental working practice, process and procedures. It is very rare for individuals to act from malice but we must recognise it can happen.

The Australian open disclosure project* identified that patients involved in a complaint seek awareness of patient safety incidents which affect them, acknowledgement of distress they have suffered, a sincere and compassionate statement of regret, a factual explanation of what has happened and a clear plan of

---

*www.health.qld.gov.au. Is a useful website for detail of this project and other relevant work going on in Australia. This is well worth a browse.

what can be done medically to redress or repair the harm done. Patients are more likely to forgive errors when apology and explanations are timely and thoughtful. Being open decreases the trauma felt by patients and may reduce litigation costs.

The benefits for the staff of due and appropriate process is the satisfaction that the communication is handled appropriately, an improvement in the understanding of occurrences from the patient's perspective, the knowledge that lessons learned will help prevent recurrence and ultimately a professional reputation for handling difficult situations well. This is a key skill for leaders to develop.

Take Home Messages

- **Value feedback positive and negative**
- **Learning lessons from feedback**
- **Changing practice as a result**

CHAPTER 10

Difficult Situations or Difficult People? Is it Me?

Consider

- **Motivation and satisfaction**
- **Resilience**
- **Difficult colleagues**
- **Strategies**

Nobody has said clinical leadership is a bed of roses. Nobody has said actions are understood and appreciated. Nobody has said the leader will feel valued and rewarded for his efforts. So why do clinicians subject themselves to these roles? As we discussed earlier there are lots of reasons and various motivations for doing so. Reward is not just about money and it is recognised that financial reward may not be a persuasive motivator in a situation where individual's basic human needs are not at stake. A need for change, new and stimulating different challenges and making a difference are all aspects of the motivation. However the reward may be the satisfaction of having achieved a transformation in the service. Reward may be having improved service quality or patient safety through a long and complex process involving information analysis and significant negotiation with colleagues. This may be the sort of reward one hugs to one's self in a moment of personal warmth rather than the stuff of public or even professional recognition. In other words the motivation and satisfaction have got to be principally personal. You have got to be the one who wants to do this. It can be a rocky road and you need personal resilience and personal determination to get there. This can not be imposed upon you.

The challenges of delivering changes in service through transformation can be large in volume but also complex and personally demanding in terms of holding information, understanding perceptions and sensitivities and steering a pathway which will keep the majority of colleagues on board. Those who are not on board can be destructive in a number of ways. They can fail to comply. This may be lack of engagement or even attendance. This manifests itself as a 'head in the sand' attitude by pretending this is not happening through lack of awareness or disregarding communication channels. It can be more active non cooperation or frank resistance or attempts to torpedo. Whatever, it is best avoided if at all possible. Identification of stakeholders and their objectives, concerns and sensitivities allows some anticipation in relation to this important aspect of progressing an agenda.

Passion in opposition should be interpreted with caution. This is not necessarily purely destructive. Typically it does mean that a colleague feels strongly about the issue under discussion and if his energies can be converted to support through addressing his particular aspect of concern he is likely to be engaged and a valuable ally.

While it is easy to say and not always easy to achieve it is good to separate the issue from the personality. A clinical leader will champion a particular service enhancement or development. He will be seen as wedded to his desire to progress this and potentially it will be seen as 'his project'. Those who do not, initially, warm to the change in service direction may be critical of the project and quite personal in their criticism and comment. It is common for the clinical leader's knowledge of the service enhancement to be challenged as out with his specialty or sphere of knowledge by others who have a closer professional link. This can be a blatant attempt to discredit the leadership and may amount to not just professional challenge but personal integrity challenge also. By discrediting the leader the project is discredited by proxy. As well as being personally hurtful this is unnecessary and unhelpful. How can this be avoided when a passionate detractor is on a roll of criticism?

Focus on the issue rather than the personality of the leader or the leader's specific knowledge. Leaders will often have responsibilities which have a greater span than their own clinical professional knowledge so as a group need coping skills. Integrity in relation to this is vital for the leader who should not pretend to have in-depth knowledge and neither is it needed specifically in relation to service transformation which will involve large and often multi-disciplinary groups who do hold that knowledge. The leader has the generic system transformation skills and that is what he brings to the table.

A useful device is to set the meeting room up in such a way that the issue may be written on a board or screen at one end of the room and all are facing it (including the leader). The leader is not therefore in a teacher/class position in the room and the construct can not be that they will seek answers which they may deem right or wrong. Rather all are addressing the issue on the wall. All are seen to have a valid set of views in relation to it. Each should be respected. Ideally a facilitator leads the discussion and the leader is in listening mode. The facilitator takes away all the information which can be documented on 'post its' by headline and the leader and facilitator can subsequently assimilate it.

Another useful approach is to lay out the problem to the organisation rather than present a solution which has been formed or 'dreamed up' earlier and outside the meeting. That approach is excluding. Laying out the problem and asking for thoughts, required information upon which to make decisions and ideas can be surprisingly fruitful. It is much less contentious and less likely to lead to personal criticism or negativity. However we do live in the real world so always be prepared for this.

At the back of your mind a small question should be asked of yourself. Am I being difficult or could I be perceived as being so. (Is it me?) If the answer is yes do consider why. It may be about approach and the interface with colleagues. Take a step back and reconsider this. Sometimes it is important to do a piece of work with individual colleagues to generate a basis for progressing. Start small. Remember passion in promoting an agenda however laudible may not be shared. The last think you want is to be seen to be ramming your own views down colleagues throats. This will have a negative impact.

Take Home Messages

- Divorce the issue from the person/personality
- Frame the issue
- Integrity and resilience
- Respect and seek different views
- Be prepared

CHAPTER 11

Clinical Engagement

Consider

- **Stages of engagement**
- **Attitudes to change**
- **Creating the appetite for change**

There are various stages to be gone through in terms of being ready to change.

- Background information
- Considering and emotional engagement
- Preparation e.g. required skills and knowledge contemplation
- Vision
- Action plan
- Maintenance phase e.g. support, performance management and recognition systems
- Revisit through audit and refresh e.g. attitude and beliefs

Clearly each stage has its needs and wants as far as individuals are concerned. Not all of a group of individuals will be at the same stage of thinking for each issue.

Individuals have different rates of adopting innovation. Interestingly we all have areas where we are early adopters and others where we lag behind peers and friends. The use of mobile phones, text messaging, predictive text messaging and satellite navigation systems in our cars are common examples.

E Rogers *Diffusion of Innovation curve described in 1995 gives some percentage values for the typical adopter behaviour

- Innovators 2.5%
- Early Adopters 13.5%
- Early Majority 34%
- Late Majority 34%
- Laggards 16%

Many of you will have read Malcolm Gladwell's excellent book The Tipping Point.[†] This also lays out the case for influencing and at what point the innovation is accepted and inevitable. The book has achieved large sales and if best seller status mean it can be bought at every air port and book shop it has that status. It is a fascinating observational description of human behaviour. We are all interested in that and this is reflected in sales.

So where does the leader fit into this? Do we have to accept that it will all take time and only some people will be amenable

---

*Rogers, EM (2003) Diffusion of Innovations (5th edn.) New York. Free Press.
†Malcolm Gladwell (2000) The Tipping Point: How Little Things Can Make a Big Difference (1st edn.), Little Brown.

to influence? Up to a point we do. However it is important to recognise that we can influence the speed of adoption or the move through the various stages. That is the mission of the leader.

It is always easier to attract individuals to a concept than to force them into change. Aim for attraction rather than compelling therefore!

Stages of individual attitude to change can be described as

- Ignorance
- Refusal
- Submission
- Tolerance
- Permission
- Passive Support
- Champion of Change
- Leadership of Change

Basically this is the same information as presented earlier in a slightly different format. Both lay out the agenda for the clinical leader in terms of influence and support of colleagues.

Ignorance, and indeed sceptisism, can be eliminated by good communication of the vision and the plan together with background information with all the caveats we have put in place earlier. These should also address the concerns and sensitivities of the group through listening to their views, aspirations and anxieties. When individuals have had their opportunity to lay all of this out and are involved in the future plan development they are less likely to resist it. Passionate argument means the speaker has strongly held views yes, but also cares and wants to be heard. Harnessing this through involvement in strategic development is the ideal. Early wins with a small step in the project may create their own momentum. Both for those who have the wins who find this encouraging but also for the disinterested and interested observer who may want assurance of success (and to avoid failure) but also not want to be left behind. Human beings are complex animals and saving face is a clinical professional behaviour as well as one used by the politicians. Nobody wants to feel they have exposed themselves to failure in a public forum through alignment to an 'unachievable' aim.

There are phases of consideration of adoption and developing action.

- Perceived need
- Solution consideration and exploration
- Solution refinement through evaluation
- Identified action

Presentation of the need for change is an interesting phenomenon. Don Berwick who has done enormous amounts of work in relation to service transformation and patient safety through his organisation the Institute of Healthcare Improvement, Boston Mass, USA* based, indicates that there are various reactions to challenging data

- The data is wrong
- The data is right, but it is not a real problem

---

*www.ihi.org. Is the web site for the Institute of healthcare Improvement and a valuable resource for individual and group advice for clinical leadership. Do explore it.

- The data is right, it's a real problem but it is not my problem
- The data is right and its my problem

The leader has to steer his colleagues through this pathway also anticipating the challenges in relation to applicability of bench-marked data and in relation to their case mix and case load for instance.

There are multiple reasons for lack of engagement:

- Denial that the status quo is unacceptable to patients
- It can all seem too difficult
- We can be uncertain how to tackle it
- It may not feel like just 'our problem'
- Others are walking away
- The status quo is not too uncomfortable
- Colleagues may not want change
- We do not want to make life uncomfortable for ourselves
- We do not want to make ourselves unpopular
- We do not want to disadvantage ourselves for promotion or awards
- We do not want to make life uncomfortable for others
- We are just too busy doing the 'day job'
- This is not my job; somebody else should 'sort it out'

In any given situation there will be a range of reasons why we should not tackle a service improvement. The above list is by no means exhaustive but it does give a feel for what the service improver may experience in terms of reception for a new way of working or service change. Some or all these thoughts and emotions may influence colleague engagement. Some individuals may have a number of reasons for not engaging. The reason given for this may not be the one that is really the 'show stopper' for them. They may not be actually aware of what that reason is e.g. discomfort and the sense of 'rocking the boat' of their existence. Or the reason may not be politically correct e.g. resistance to a patient improvement. Or they may have an ambition which they are pursuing and their perception that involvement might jeopodise that e.g. application for an academic post, an educational role or an award. Individuals feel they are best placed to decide what is best for them and their career and this belief will be unshakable. However, as we know, there are always different perspectives.

Our clinical leader may know or speculate on the reasons for lack of engagement. An awareness of the multilayered agendas of clinical colleagues does place him well to identify these and try to craft his service improvement in such a way that there is an advantage for specific individuals to be involved. This may be quite time consuming and involve individual negotiation and discussion but it is time well spent.

Take Home Messages

- **Communication is all**
- **Build on small wins**
- **Attract to change versus force**
- **Listen**
- **Tipping points**

CHAPTER 12

Influencing and Negotiation

Consider

- **Working with people versus 'doing it to them'**
- **Understanding concerns**
- **Communicate to understand**

We have considered how to approach a service change, we have considered identifying our stakeholders and their aspirations and our approach to this. What about next steps? We have identified that laying a problem in front of the team or group of colleagues and approaching the problem as one that you will work with them on jointly is a good approach. They do not want to feel they are 'having this done to them'. Self determination and control of one's destiny is very important to self esteem and self worth. The opportunity to have their concerns taken account of and thoughts how the future should be shaped at a strategic level are valuable. They may also be able to identify the steps necessary to get there and what the potential obstacles and unintended consequences might be. These guys hold the answer. They know their service better than anybody else.

However sometimes there is a strategic direction of travel which feels like a big step. This may be a political imperative or be (worst case scenario) seen as a financial expedient and colleagues may feel they wish to resist the change on patient safety grounds. This is laudable and understandable. Nobody wants to put the patient at risk or reduce the quality of the service they deliver. Examples of this might be moving a service into a community setting or increasing the use of extended role allied healthcare professionals in delivering elements of service. These situations are potentially contentious and not the way things have been done in the past.

The role of the clinical leader is to understand the concerns of colleagues; to actually visibly write down the points. This simple step often is a good indication that colleagues that they are being listened to. 'That is an important/interesting point. Let me make a note of it...'

Some anxieties and concerns are valid and do need attention to detail in addressing them. Importantly, having considered the specifics, it is vital that there is feedback to colleagues about the pieces of work which will be undertaken to address their issue. This might be about sourcing information that is available or performing audits. For example the issue of role extension of radiographers into ultrasound practice involves formal training courses which are accredited. They have mentoring aspects and they work with radiologists to build up expertise but also trust and respect for the role extended colleagues practice. These individuals do have medico legal responsibility for their own practice. Radiologists having this information and understanding the working practice feel in a better position to support the extended role practitioner and their place in service delivery.

Other concerns have relatively simple solutions. It may be that there is knowledge or information which colleagues need to understand the situation fully. Information is power. These are intelligent people. They can process information and come to conclusions. They do however need to respect the source and quality of the data and see it as valid to their own situation. Anticipation of the need for this might allow some colleague engagement in defining the required dataset.

True reflection of practice through valid and respected information is very powerful. The story of the frog is now in common usage. If you have not heard it it is quite compelling. If you put a frog in a pan of cold water and put it on the stove and switch the heat on under it. The water will get hot. The frog will make no effort to leave the pan. Eventually the water will boil and the frog will explode. The metaphor is frogs do not have the ability to detect small changes in temperature. We can not be in that position as leaders. We need to understand our systems through processes which give us trends and identify outlying performance, individuals or service. This allows us to benchmark with other services and inform change. If we can not measure something we do not know the impact of any improvement or indeed if it is an improvement. We need to be able to detect change.

In considering a service development it is important to consider exactly what we are trying to improve. Importantly also how we will know if there has been an improvement. This is done by identifying the data that needs to be gathered to inform this and a means of gathering it.

The other powerful tool in the box is process mapping of a service. This involves getting the whole team who provide a service gathered together. This should include not just medial and nursing staff but also allied health professionals, receptionists and porters. It is best to involve other stakeholders including service managers, those interacting and referring to the service from primary and secondary care but fundamentally importantly the users of the service. That is the patient or patients and potentially their parents or carers.

The process is then to describe the journey of the patient from first contact with healthcare to delivery of final outcome. This is then mapped up on the wall on large sheets of paper as steps in the journey. The journey initially will involve the journey of the paper request referring the patient to the service, appointment arrangement but finally the journey steps will involve the patient themselves and subsequently reports or letters and therefore again paper or patient information transfer.

The team should be facilitated by a non team member who understands the process and can support and encourage the team through this. The whole team should sit facing the wall with the journey map on it. At each step the key constraints in the service are discussed. Everybody has a contribution. Each is valid. The secretarial and portering contribution may be absolutely pivotal to identifying where service is not flowing and why. The key player is, however, the patient. They are at the receiving end of the service and interface with it in all its parts. Their views and perspectives are really illuminating. These can be quite unexpected and potentially challenging. Examples of this might be the black hole of communication they feel with some services. The holding of a perception of lack of knowledge as to where they are in the system or the queue. Being repeatedly asked for their demographic details underlines this perception.

We all like to think we are providing a good and efficient service. It is potentially uncomfortable to hear of some patient's experiences. However this is married with the patient as a resource for the next step in conjunction with colleagues. Small pieces of work are done considering what would improve each key constraint and what the impact would be and if there are unexpected consequences or collateral. The patient is a useful sounding board. Large department chain stores need market research and engagement with their potential customers to do needs assessment. For strange reasons not apparent to me healthcare has not seen the need to do that as a modus operandi. Rather paternalistic assumptions have been made with the very best of intentions in most cases.

Married with process mapping is the need to understand the service. We can only do that through robust data and information. The work of the Institute of Healthcare Improvement show cases various types of methodology.* This is best gathered by those in the service and to agreed definitions. The definitions are important to ensure reproducibility but also for benchmarking and aggregation. The elements of this are

- Demand
- Capacity

---

* www.ihi.org.

- Activity
- Queue

Typically what we have measured historically is activity and potentially saturated activity. This is not useful information.

Demand for a service is the true demand. All may not progress through the entire patient journey but will need 'work' to filter and make the decision. Therefore this work should be acknowledged and factored into any service redesign recognizing this is valid activity.

Capacity is not only the number of clinical slots, available theatre sessions, out patient slots or CT scan slots. Each of these requires availability of equipment or accommodation but also availability of staff. For instance if a surgeon is on holiday his clinical room or theatre slots will be available but he will not be. This is not true available capacity. In the event of maintenance the CT scanner will not be available but the scanning team of radiographers and radiologists will be. The capacity is not there. A holistic view of all elements of necessary capacity is required.

Activity is what we are actually delivering in terms of units of care e.g. scans or operations.

The queue is how many people are waiting.

The backlog is for how long.

I have heard it said that demand is what we should be doing, activity what we are doing, capacity what we could be doing and queue or backlog what we should have done.

Ideally having got this information we match up our capacity and demand to identify if we have a match, if we have enough capacity to meet the demand on the service or if we need to consider how we extend our capacity. In order to do this we have to have a common currency to measure these parameters. Time is the common currency often. In the instance of clinic slots we need to work out (with a stop watch) what the average time is for the consultation. What the longest and shortest times are (the outliers) and understand if they are related to particular diagnostic or disease or conditions. If so is there an element of predictability. We then need to consider the overall availability of the clinic room and the staffing necessary for it to run. This will allow us to know what our daily capacity is. This can then be aggregated to weekly, monthly annual etc. It can also be done by hospital, region and even nationally if necessary.

In terms of demand for a service the number of requests for the service are counted and these then converted into the average time for clinic slots to give an aggregated overall view of demand. Again the opportunity presents itself to consider if we have the capacity to deal with the demand. Our activity is what we are doing. Measuring this can be by patient numbers and/or slot numbers. We also know what the backlog is in terms of how long patients are waiting to get to the clinic. This can also be converted to the common currency of time and we know how many clinical slots we need.

Let us consider this for a day for simplicity. If we get an average of 10 requests for service on a given day and we have 10 clinical slots all is well if we have no late additions or emergencies. If we only have 8 slots and a demand for 10 per day we have a deficit on a daily basis and will build up a waiting list. If we have 12 slots and a daily demand of 10 we are wasting capacity.

The reality is more complex but this gives a feel for the methodology. Ideally services should function at about 85% of full capacity for efficient working according to IHI.

Having done the exercise and scoped the service consideration can be given to improved performance. This is a quality issue and a patient safety issue ensuring timely access to services. It is also a financial governance issue ensuring good husbandry of resource and best value for money. The latter argument will not necessarily be seen as a valid driver for change in the eyes of colleagues who may be cynical about financial motivation and consider the improvement proposal is a cost cutting exercise.

So what can be done to improve service where there are key constraints identified?

Help is at hand. The Modernisation Agency in England and the Scottish Government Collaborative Programmes have done a lot of work on this. High Impact Changes have been identified which have worked. These are well documented and available widely. They have also published Case Studies.* These are illuminating local assessments of service key constraints. The method of identification of these and what was done to improve the service together with information and data to support this is documented. In addition and helpfully the detail of which department has done this in which healthcare area and contact details are available. This is useful information which is freely available.

Suffice it to say the impact has improved the service access for patients, the quality of service through patient engagement

---

*www.scotland.gov.uk/Topics/Health/NHS-Scotland/Delivery-Improvement.

and also reduced pressure in services with staff and whole system benefit.

Take Home Messages

- **Acknowledge concerns**
- **Respect contributions as valid and valued**
- **Communicate and inform**
- **Value patient input**

CHAPTER 13

Service Transformation

Consider

- **Changing world, changing demographics, changing needs of service**
- **Challenge traditional provision**
- **Predictive planning**

Clinical leaders are living in exciting times. Innovation of treatment, diagnostic facilities and capabilities are constantly progressing. The service is quite unrecognisable from that provided, for instance, at the inception of the UK National Health Service in 1948. Outcomes are better, patient safety is improved and the quality of service constantly under scrutiny for improvement opportunity. Of course resource is an issue. This is true both in terms of money and manpower. Both are in short supply and need careful husbandry.

As the population lives longer there is more pressure on services from age related disease. Whilst we are seeing an increase in cardiovascular disease and cancer demands on the service is also generated by long term conditions providing significant challenge in service provision. Examples of this are arthritis and diabetes.

In the first half of the twentieth Century the health concern was infection. Antibiotics and better living conditions and standards revolutionised this. In the second half of the twentieth Century the challenge was acute disease and our health services were geared up to deliver acute care. As we move further into the twenty first Century it is increasingly clear that the challenge will be providing care for long term conditions. Our services are geared to acute provision and not really fit for purpose. If we always do what we have always done we will always get what we always had it is said. As service leaders we do need to take a step back and consider how we do provide the service and challenge traditional methods and conventional wisdom. This is an ongoing exercise but absolutely necessary to the future of health provision nationally and internationally. This is going to need many clinical leaders and they are going to need to be brave. The service needs significant reprofiling and patient and public education will form part of this.

Service improvement has been dictated by individual changes in practice or improvements in equipment. By way of example in radiology a quiet revolution has taken place over the last quarter century with the introduction of general ultrasound following on the success of foetal assessment. This was followed hard on the heels with CT and MRI and most recently Positron Emission Tomography (PET) scanning. Departments have had to extend, space has had to be created and the workforce extended and trained. There have been implications for Higher Education Institutions and accrediting bodies in terms of keeping up and anticipating change in order to arm the workforce for action. All this has taken management, yes, but also a vision, a generated sense of direction and a goal that the service can get behind. Leadership has been fundamental to this.

Has this been welcome? Of course patients benefit from the increased diagnostic capacity, the ability to diagnose and stage their disease prior to surgery. Historically open surgery may have been needed for this. Disease can be monitored and early warnings of adverse features identified. There is patient benefit.

Referring clinicians do value the enhanced capability to extend the scope of their own practice and the service they deliver.

The staff delivering the service have tremendous job satisfaction that they are delivering the cherished service which is required. They know they are making a difference to individual patients and to the overall patient population and therefore public health.

Recruitment to radiology as a profession from junior doctors recently had the highest ratio of applicants of any speciality in Scotland and I believe in the UK.

This is an example of comprehensive service transformation. It has been successful in the eyes of all the stakeholders above. Of course it is an expensive service and will develop further but it is an example of whole system transformation.

We have changed services in an arguably random and incremental way historically. We have done some of the elements of service transformation. These are articulated by the Institute of Healthcare Improvement as:

- Structural change
- Process simplification and redesign
- System redesign
- Transformation

The scope:

- Consideration of a single service or process
- Multiple processes
- Network rethinking
- Rethinking of healthcare delivery

The drivers:

- Hit an annual target
- Greater improvement
- Effective practice
- Best in class

So how do clinical leaders shift up a gear from what we have done to what we need to do? Summarising the thinking we have explored he should consider:

- Articulate the vision: state the aims
- Get ownership of the vision: in isolation this will not work
- Seductive examples and evidence from reputable, credible sources

- Small wins to build on
- Sharing learning
- WIIFM*
- Build on positive relationships
- Good practice used to influence
- Peer pressure tipping point
- Early adopters to laggards

When there is a wind in the sails you do not need an engine. The metaphor is that active engagement has its own momentum and is the best approach if it can be achieved. It is easier to push than to pull. If colleagues are attracted to an idea they are more likely to engage. Think of attractors which will be helpful to progress of a project. They may not be immediately obvious to the whole team.

Take Home Messages

- **Take a step back and consider need**
- **Create a vision for the future**
- **Plan for this**
- **Active engagement has its own momentum**

---

*I will explain!

CHAPTER 14

Negotiation and WIIFM

Consider

- The difference between need and want
- Collaborative advantage; Is competition necessary?
- Communicate
- The long term relationship

We are all human and we are all persuaded of the need to change or do something if there is an advantage for us. That therefore is an important point in progressing a negotiation.

WIIFM = What's in it for me?

Fundamental to a negotiation is an understanding of the stakeholders and their requirements. This may be groups of referrers e.g. general practitioners or it might be an individual role extended practitioner, surgeon, secretary or porter. It is said we all have basic human needs. These are around heat, food warmth and so on. We, in addition, do have wants. These are the aspects that make life worth living. If 'needs' are the bicycle 'wants' are the bells and whistles. Negotiation is not around 'needs' but is around 'wants' typically.

It is nobody's wish to come out of a negotiation situation crushed and completely defeated. This is an acceptable situation if you are buying a car or selling your house and want a great deal and do not care about the future relationship with the other party. However in a long term relationship this is a very unhelpful position for all parties. In a long term relationship, which service delivery is, we aim to try for the win: win situation. Everybody comes away with some benefit. It may not be everything they want but they are not coming away 'empty handed'. It is important to decide at the outset what the back stop position is and feel able to manoeuver towards it but not beyond it. In other words what are the absolute 'needs' of the situation or essentials and what are the 'wants' desirable but non essential extras. Feel able to lose 7:4 as one colleague put it. Do not die in a ditch or 'burn' over non essential elements you can live without if the other party feels strongly about them. There may be major implications for them and limited implication for you. The full understanding of both parties should be explored in detail so all requirements are understood before getting to this position. The very discussion around detail of what can be changed and 'boxing and coxing' and juggling around a negotiated outcome can be bonding for future relationships.

The other thing to consider is negotiation need not be seen as adversarial. In fact it need not be adversarial. Collaboration is a comfortable way of developing and supporting a long

term relationship with stakeholders. To decide if this approach can be adopted it is as well to consider the 'collaborative advantage' to each individual or party in going down that route. What is in it for them to collaborate rather than be in competition? If a core of collaborative advantage can be identified this can be exploited to advantage. This makes a very solid basis for future negotiation and joint working. We are all in the business of providing healthcare and unless we are actually bidding against each other for a service, collaboration is likely to have distinct advantages for us and for the patient. Actually, even when we are bidding against each other it is worth considering if competition is the appropriate way forward.

Going back to the issue of perception we all approach problems from our own perspective. This means applying our thinking and system of beliefs and values to it through our style. It means applying our experience of past work and general life situations to it in a positive sense. If one is thinking negatively then we all have our baggage. To every perception there is another interpretation. This is captured in the glass half full: glass half empty term in common usage. Some typically do approach life with thinking the best of the facts and reality they see in front of them whilst others are concerned about the future implications, risks and potential for difficulty. Each of these individuals may be frustrated by the other's commentary around any situation. 'They are too up beat...' or 'they are always negative'. In fact both views are valid and helpful in forming a holistic view but different approaches are needed for each. Acknowledgement of the upbeat view whilst introducing a reality of potential risk is a useful approach and conversely introducing a positive list of benefits currently experienced and future positive potential benefit is helpful. This is defined as flexing your style. This allows matching of the situation to the needs of the individuals or groups through approach. There is no dishonesty just acknowledgement of difference, valuing that input and recognising how each will feel most engaged and give of their best.

Another aspect of negotiation which requires attention is the confirmation of understanding of the position of each party including their context, anxieties and aspirations. Once again the leader should never assume his perception is the same as others but should reflect back their requirements in his own words to ensure he has understood and give the other party the opportunity to do the same. A personal example of this was a line manager colleague who was to sign off a study leave form which involved funding. I had not expected this to be a prob-lem but it was rejected. I tried to understand why through discussion. I was concerned that he thought I was trying to cheat the system. He explained that the funding required nego-tiation and he did not want to be the person to do this but that rather I do this before approaching him. He did not want to do the extra work. We had both interpreted the situation in differ-ent ways and discussion was necessary to understand the truth which was entirely satisfactory for both of us when we under-stood the perspectives. The frustration we both felt was dissipated by achieving a shared understanding.

Around service improvement, negotiating engagement of colleagues can be challenging for the clinical leader. Again, considering your audience is important. The Director of Finance will have a different outcome need and set of yardsticks and milestones from clinicians. The financial imperative is, of course, important. We may all wish it was not and feel idealistic about doing things in the face of expense but idealism is not reality. In negotiation with the Director of Finance (who will share these values with the Chief Executive) financial prudence will need to be seen to be addressed. However clinical colleagues may find it easy to reject a project that is founded on finance and saving. They will however be persuaded by patient safety, clinical risk profiles especially if there is credible evidence behind it. Match the presentation of facts and aims to the audience. This, again, is not dishonesty but recognition that in complex situations the aims of projects and service transformations are multilayered and must work at all levels to mobilise all the necessary support. The situation has been described as bilingual. Cost and quality are two sides of the same coin in the analogy.

We identify key stakeholders and consider strategies for identifying their needs and the way they would like the issues put across. We do this at a conscious and unconscious level. We can, in some instances see a sponsor of the project who will be an ally. This may be formal executive sponsorship which will open doors for the clinical leader or it may be an influential colleague whose support will influence others. This is not necessarily at an operational or involved level but rather by a few well placed words. Often senior colleagues have the respect of their peers and their 'approval' of a development can be empowering for the team taking it forward. Of course the converse is true. These 'opinion formers' will need to be nurtured and cultured. This must be done with integrity or will be seen as a sham and rejected by them and watching peers. We all want others to have a good opinion of us and our actions. It is helpful if these are endorsed.

The value of personal and professional networks to support service developments is recognised. These can be formal through professional organisations or be individuals we have been at college with, play golf with, trained with or worked on other projects with. Building coalitions and alliances is an investment in the future.

In healthcare we need to consider what incentives and inducements there are for teams to engage in specific service changes. In doing this the down side needs acknowledgement and managed if we are to maintain credibility.

Integrity is a valued commodity. The leader develops trust of others through demonstration of consistency and honourable action. This is based on how he does his business on a day to day basis. He should be aware he is a role model and is being observed. His actions will be considered by others. This is information they will use when considering their future involvement with him. Interface and communication with others is therefore vitally important in content and style.

Take Home Messages

- **Flex your style; consider your audience**
- **Understand perspective**
- **Listen**
- **Nurture allies**
- **Have integrity**

CHAPTER 15

Communication

Consider

- **Audience needs and wants**
- **Media strategies**
- **Adverse impacts**
- **Presentation skills**

Of course communication happens in many ways formal and informal, verbal and written not to mention visual and observational. Some of those adopted in healthcare setting as are:

- Management briefings to staff
- Workshops
- E-mail
- Face to face
- Newsletters
- Websites
- Post

For some, service transformations are of such significance and magnitude that all these approaches will be used. On other occasions the issues require selective communication and lesser distribution.

Leadership will involve considering who needs to know and why:

- For strategic awareness
- For action; planning
- For action: delivery
- For awareness for unexpected consequences good and bad
- For awareness for interest

Strategic awareness may be in relation to letting the chief executive know about some form of adverse incident which has the potential for media, police or external regulatory agency attention. This is not about concealing the issue but forearming the chief executive who may have to field questions and commission an internal review of circumstances. He may also be the person fronted up to the television camera and will value early warning to allow preparation. A culture of 'no surprises' is helpful.

Dealing with the media is best considered with caution. They have a different agenda from the healthcare services. They are in the business of developing stories for newspapers or television. They want to have something to sell and have the potential to sensationalise what might be an unfortunate set of circumstances for an individual patient, member of staff or a service. It is probably true to say good news stories about healthcare are much less common in the press and on television than adverse publicity. Where at all possible have the in-house, trained communication staff with you if you have to give an interview. If your organisation does not have that resource take advice and attend a formal media training course to arm yourself with strategies to cope in what can be a pressured situation. A device when a difficult question is asked is to give your self a breathing space to think by saying 'Ah, that is an interesting point and you may think that but…' and then give your own view of the situation. This also allows a way into presenting prepared and well considered material. You are in control under these circumstances.

It is not always possible to get sight of newspaper copy before it goes to print but it is always worth offering to check for the medical terms and accuracy. This can be couched in terms of support to ensure the complex situation is clear to the reporter. They may just be grateful! Another approach is to give them a sheet of paper or briefing note detailing the relevant issues, background, approach that is being taken, challenges and likely outcomes and timescales or answers to whatever the particular question is likely to be. They will still want to interview you but they may (on a good day) augment that with what you have given them and what you know to be appropriate and accurate.

In this day and age communication is fast and instant. The media do not have space to manoeuver and they often do not give much time for consideration. Just be aware of this before agreeing to be interviewed.

The need to have information for planning and action is clear. Awareness of unexpected and unintended consequences is an interesting one. The services who are hosting a particular development may be very enthusiastic about it and gathered in the momentum of delivering it. They may have, in all good faith, considered stakeholders and all other aspects of a new patient benefit they intend to deliver. They may, however, not have foreseen that their service development may increase the need for blood sample analysis in the lab to monitor the improvement. The lab may have been unaware of this impact and become aware only as a result of increased and unexpected activity. This is usually unwelcome and a difficult situation to retrieve. Anticipation is all. The concept of matched clinical change is a good one. This can be a structured approach within organisations where any planned service development is highlighted to all departments at an early stage to allow stakeholders to be identified formally rather than at the discretion of the host development service. This can be a formalised step in the planning process and discharged through a simple device like a check list.

Failure to identify a stakeholder can be an oversight and is regrettable. It can however be deliberate and to make a service development seem affordable when potentially it has wide financial consequences. A formal checklist approach obviates this concern.

We have discussed the format of meeting for engagement and the importance of not presenting solutions but achieving engagement through sharing the problem and developing the solution in partnership with the group. For the leader 'walk humble' is good advice. Be in listening mode and value all contributions. Tailor the information to the particular audience.

For individual clinical communication between colleagues the Institute of Healthcare Improvement has a format. This is SBAR*

- Situation
- Background

---

*www.ihi.org. As the website of the Institute of Healthcare Improvement gives detailed examples of the use of this tool and many others. Well worth a visit.

- Assessment
- Recommendations

This is a useful way of considering what information is to be given in other contexts and ensuring all aspects are covered. This has resonance in both clinical and other communication situations.

Some of us are more confident than others in standing up and delivering lectures and presenting information. Some have happy extrovert styles that lend themselves to that way of operating. Despite this clinical leaders who are less comfortable with this aspect of the role may have to stand and deliver. Is there any advice?

It is said that public speaking is like learning to drive. At our first lesson we think we will never master all the instructions, things to check, hand eye co-ordination and getting from A to B. But hey most of us drive and by the way can chat at the same time and even change the channel of the radio whilst doing so. We got there. Public speaking is in that same arena. In the same way that some pass the driving test first time others need more practice. Presentation delivery is like that too.

Being prepared is pretty important. Know your audience and pitch appropriately to their level of knowledge and understanding. Know what you want to say. Consider how you will say it and construct your talk. Winston Churchill is said to have rehearsed his speeches exhaustively. Well it certainly worked for him! Consider how you will deliver. Yes practice! Ensure you keep to time. Dragging on too long is irritating for the audience and a discourtesy to the next speaker. Always seek some feedback or evaluation of your performance. This can be quite informal. 'How do you think it went? Did I manage to get my point over ok?...'

Another aspect of communication is style. This can range from the most formal memo from on high to chatting over coffee. It may be the reason for communicating is giving information and no engagement with the receiver is needed or intended. However it is fair to say the more personal the communication the more the receiver will feel engaged, involved and valued. Catching a colleague in the corridor and passing on information as an unplanned act may be valued by some recipients as opportunistic. Others will take the view that if they had not met you by chance they would not have been given the information which they felt it their right to have. Is this a no win situation? The consideration here is to plan ahead and try to be appropriate rather than haphazard. Standing and preaching is likely to be received negatively (shades of the headmaster pupil relationship). Individuals like to be treated as responsible adults and where at all possible individuals. If urgent transmission of information to a large group has to take a less personal approach acknowledging the lack of individual contact at the start is useful e.g. 'I am sorry to send out an impersonal memo about this important issue but as you will recognise time is at a premium and I am relying on your help and support to take this forward urgently and wanted to waste no time in making you aware of the specifics...'

Finally giving information for interest is actually very important in terms of valuing staff members. Knowledge is power. Staff do not want to read about a major service transformation in the local evening newspapers and have no previous knowledge of it. This is embarrassing for them in discussion with relatives and neighbours. However little they may be involved directly having the awareness of the service development is valued. It is a way in which organisations can show they value their staff, it is good internal communication.

Take Home Messages

- **Preparation and anticipation**
- **Consider your audience**
- **Listen**
- **Seek feedback and involvement in solution development from the audience**

CHAPTER 16

Committees

Consider

- **Skills for the chair**
- **Strategy to achieve outcomes**
- **The role and remit of committee its members and chair**

Committees are another forum of communication. This is typically a group activity and around an agenda.

Formal agenda setting is time well spent. Typically this is done by the chairman and secretary of the committee and is based on the minute of the previous meeting, standing items that the committee consider e.g. reports from other committees, complaints profiles etc and new business. It is always worth having a section on information and papers for noting. This should be explicit as the committee then understand these will not be discussed unless there is some exceptional reason why but that they have been included in their circulation for their background information or action. Again if it is action this should be made clear. The chairman has a responsibility to ensure the agenda is covered and the group not sidetracked but also to ensure that all perspectives are covered. All voices that have a view should be heard and that he who shouts loudest should not drown everybody else out. Sharing out of 'air time' for different perspectives is a chairman prerogative but also a skill. Use this wisely and it will gain respect.

Chairmanship is a skill like any other. Practice and observing others whom one regards as good chairmen to check approach and what works for them is useful. A lot of skills can be learned by observation. Keeping cool under fire is helpful. Heated discussion may reflect passionate views but it may stifle the timid with an alternative and valid view. They will then feel resentful and not committed to the decision. This is to be avoided. If the committee can be viewed as a meeting of minds and ideas with valid challenge this is helpful. Reflection aiming at consensus where possible but informed decision where not works well.It is most likely that individuals will accept the committee decision this way. The chairman in summarising committee discussion and decision has the benefit of having the last word and focusing the decision. This can be very helpful.

The remit of a committee is best to be explicit and the chairman can refer the group to this and their role as a focusing exercise. We all have busy lives and it is helpful to tackle only what is expected and not stray into cul de sacs which may be time thieves. Likewise committee members need to understand their role. If they are representative of colleagues they may need to refer to their constituency before a decision is made. They may have professional alliances. As a group it is ideal if the committee can accept that wide ranging discussion can take place round the committee. All views are heard but when the decision is made members stick to that and do not try to reopen the argument. This is not always possible but is an ideal to aim for. Explicit expectation of this can be made by the chairman.

It is a responsibility of the chairman to reflect back to the committee a summary of discussion and agreed outcome and actions. This can be done in quite an informal way agenda item by agenda item where there has been any significant discussion. More formal confirmation of the committee decision and agreed actions is essential when contentious topics have been discussed.

The power of the pen should not be forgotten. Well argued cases documented in a structured fashion and circulated before committees allow full and informed consideration. Some individuals prefer to assimilate information by reading and reflection and will relish the opportunity to do so. Others will place more value on the accompanying narrative at the committee meeting.

As a committee member and as chair it is important to ensure that an accurate record of the meeting is taken. It is always best for the chair to have a note taker identified at the beginning of the meeting if there is not a formal minute taker. This ensures that they take responsibility for noting important points and decisions during the meeting and do not rely on reflective memory which might be more subject to their own interpretation.

At a very basic level it is important that committee members are given detail of the date, time and venue of the meeting in plenty time to ensure they are able to make themselves available. Regular meetings benefit from a schedule of meeting dates being made available. Papers for the meeting (agenda, note of previous meeting and any accompanying papers) should be sent out well in advance to allow reading and assimilation of the information. This facilitates active involvement of committee members at the meeting. Tabled papers should be avoided if at all possible. It is really not possible to read a paper and have an informed discussion about it simultaneously.

Consider having both start and finishing times of meetings. This introduces a discipline and expectation for all participants. Some will go as far as timings for agenda items. This can be useful if individuals are coming to the committee to report on one item only. It is challenging for the chairman however.

Take Home Messages

- **Mutual respect for members of the committee**
- **Understand the outcome required**
- **Focus on outcomes and issues not behaviour**

CHAPTER 17

Followership

Consider

- **Valuing of individuals and their place in the organisation**
- **Definition of expectations**
- **Retrieval**

Followership may be a new word. Indeed I may have made it up! Is there any such thing? Do people sign up to be good followers? Of course they do not. Typically they are employed by the healthcare organisation. They have a job to do in a team or service. They understand where they fit in and are line managed and performance managed against standards. They are set tasks and targets and personal development plans may be constructed with them. They do not sign up to blind, unquestioning, faithful following! This is then an agenda for the line manager and their leader in the clinical context. The specifics of an individual's role are a microcosm of the organisation. The individual needs to see the vision of where he is to go and where that fits in the organisation. This may seem obvious but it is by no means commonplace to have that connection between individual and organisational aims. In order for an individual to feel valued this insight is important. The clinical leader can do this for the individual. Reinforcement of the individual staff member's value to the organisation through their contribution will be reinforcing for them. This builds self esteem and trust.

Again it is said that nobody comes to work to do a bad job. Everybody is doing their best. We all have days we are feeling better, have slept better or have just had a holiday. Then there are the other sort of days when there has been a bump in the car on the way in or a large bill arrived in the post or the baby was crying all night. These things are life and as humans we are all subject to them. Tolerance of individual situations is vital. However we do need to ensure standards and relative consistency. It is important that individuals are given an understanding of expectations of them and where these are not being met that they are made aware of this early on and are supported through standard setting.

The concept of institutional strategic incompetence comes to mind. This is a recent concept but one I recognise. Individuals may say 'Oh don't ask me to arrange meetings/write up the notes/arrange rotas/sort out the clinic template/write the business case... I am hopeless at that sort of thing'. Inevitably they do not get asked to do what ever it was and they establish a pattern of not doing the task(s). The impact is on the 'willing horse' who can and will take this on. Often there is no particular advantage of having done this task for the person doing it. As a leader it is good to observe behaviour of others and ensure the 'willing horse' gets a fair deal.

Self reflection of behaviour, outcomes and how situations have gone is a healthy leadership practice. Having done this move on do not dwell on what might have been. It is history. Lessons are for the future. History is in the past.

In addition to self reflection team or committee reflection is a useful exercise. Teams may find this challenging to begin with. 'Well how did that go?', 'Could we have done that in a different way?' or 'Are we focused on our remit or out of our territory?' The chair can also ask' Are you happy with the way things are going?' Once the team realise this will be a regular reflection they are ready for it and can contribute thoughtfully. This is helpful in team bonding and shows the leader to be caring and responsive through being in listening mode. Action must follow of course!

Take Home Messages

- **Clarify individual role profiles**
- **Clarify expectations**
- **Observe contributions**
- **Learn from but do not dwell on poor outcomes**

CHAPTER 18

Helping Others to Help You

Consider

- **Own way of working**
- **Communicate with secretary**
- **Agree and plan joint way of working**

I did say that this was not a generic leadership book with details of finance, budgets and planning processes but there are some things that can be useful and need consideration.

Get to know your support staff. They are more likely to go the extra mile for you if you have shown some genuine interest in them as people. They too have lives, homes, hobbies and worries and would like you to factor that into how you relate to them at various levels. Establishing this is a good investment.

Having a secretary or personal assistant is a privilege. It is worth ensuring you maximise the benefit of that. At the time you start working together arrange a time to sit down together without interruptions and distractions. Have a small agenda. Explain what your job involves. It may be that your clinical leadership role is just part of your professional responsibility and an understanding of the time commitment you have to devote to this is useful. At a very practical level your timetable should be shared. If your are involved in open heart surgery on a Tuesday morning it will be clear you are not available to take phone calls for instance as a extreme example. Establish when you have clinical leadership time, what your fixed commitments are, their frequency etc and if they involve travel or being out of the work place. Establish when you are clinically committed elsewhere and what you would choose to do about urgent matters that arise during those times e.g. bleep system to contact you, cross cover by a colleague.

Where at all possible categorise the level of issue or urgent matter which would trigger this rather than being deferred until you are available. This is not a tablet of stone but can be built up over time. It is a useful starting point and empowers your secretary who may find the decision uncomfortable without guidance especially early in your working relationship.

When you are away on leave or on business make a formal arrangement about who covers your clinical leadership responsibility. This saves time in an urgent situation and gives the secretary confidence around managing urgent and indeed routine matters. It also makes you appear efficient which is appreciated.

Sometimes the volume of e-mail traffic can seem overwhelming and very time consuming. It is also frustrating as many when opened seems to waste time and not add value or significance. The all too easy habit of copying in rafts of colleagues who may only have a peripheral interest in the topic is not a good one. I suspect we have to learn to deal with it as it is not likely to stop! Global e-mails are a particular irritation. Despite the fact that many organisations have systems in place to have editorial rights over what is allowed to be a global e-mail it often seems as if they are not of global interest and frequently not of interest at all!

Consider giving your secretary access to your e-mail. Empower her to deal with requests for meetings, print off and arrange papers for meetings and generally manage your diary commitments. You will have to lay out some ground rules for this e.g. regular specified committee meetings and one to one meetings are sacrosanct. If you have been away for a week you require time a day (or what you decide) of no appointments to catch up on return. Always ensure you give him or her advanced notice of any request for a meeting that you are very keen to attend and for which you are prepared to move other diary commitments.

Many of us have electronic diaries and our secretaries arrange meetings in that format but the systems work as well for the paper diary. Hybrid arrangements also exist where the secretary may hold an electronic diary for you but, like me, you may carry a filofax for convenience. Regular reconciliation meetings of the two diaries allow a bit of catch up with your secretary and confirming appointment priority etc. We call this 'doing the diaries'!

Consider asking your secretary to put your e-mails into files by category if you are away and you can deal with on the basis of your chosen categories of urgency on return e.g. categories could be — urgent, for information or relating to specific issues which can be predetermined.

When you do review your e-mails consider starting with the most recent as this may avoid reading through a developing string of e-mails when the final one resolves the issue. This is not to everybody's taste and akin to reading the last chapter of a book first...it does speed things up though!

These suggestions all apply to letters and paper mail which come in but few of us work in that environment exclusively these days.

Ask you secretary to set up a 'bring forward' for agendas and papers for meetings. If you are unfamiliar with the 'bring forward' it is a file system which has slots 1-31. As papers for meetings come in these can be placed in the relevant day slot and are available to put into a weekly 'bring forward' loose leave file which your secretary will make up for you at the end of the week before. It also means that if you require to see papers for a meeting on a particular day they are readily available.

Be prepared and show willing to revisit the 'way of working framework'. Initially it is as well to lay out your thoughts and preferred ways but after a period of time weeks or months perhaps it is useful to revisit this with your secretary. She may have ideas about things could be improved or streamlined drawing on her previous experience. You do not hold the monopoly on good ideas. Even after long periods of working together with your secretary she may be bashful about suggesting things that would make life easier for you or for her and make little difference to you. Do consider asking the question.

Some of us are 'power freaks' or 'control freaks' and feel the need to do everything ourselves making the most minute decisions in case the decision taken would not have been exactly the one we would have taken. I have some sympathy and understanding with this but really — give yourself a break! You do not have to decide everything you can be flexible and it does speed up processes. Think of it as a skill in delegation. It is also empowerment of your secretary and gives them confidence to support you. You set the boundaries of this so the risks are minimal and the rewards great.

Likewise for other staff the clinical leader works with e.g. project leaders etc a structured and agreed approach to communication and engagement is worthwhile and the best use of that limited commodity time.

Time is never in adequate supply. Good planning around meetings with both stop and start times together with focused agendas are helpful. Time management is about individual discipline however. Consider the overall week, fixed commitments and the time allocated to each and be individually ruthless about not being drawn into timewasting activity which does not add value. This is easier said that done. Be firm but kind! If you are not only you know when you will have to undertake the displaced activity e.g. in the evening or at the weekend which can not be an attractive proposition.

Take Home Messages

- **Plan your relationship with colleagues**
- **Consider how to maximize the benefit of joint working**
- **Keep your agreed arrangements under review**

CHAPTER 19

And Finally...

Consider

- **Look after yourself**
- **Plan your life work balance**

You must look after yourself. Ultimately only you can do that. You set the limits and boundaries on what you take on and what you do not. You set the time you come in to work and the time you go home. You decide if you take work home with you and how much 'home time' you devote to that. It is important to ensure you have life work balance. There will always be a list of things to be done. The list is never completed and signed off and that is something that has to be 'managed'. Only you can do that. We need to know when to walk away and leave things for another day both physically and mentally. Some find that easier than others.

I would be the first to say a new challenge can be very stimulating. For a clinician moving into a leadership role this can create a real sense of energy and revitalisation. It is exciting. Making a difference in a different way, using new skills and testing our abilities are all reinforced by successes. Not every day is an upbeat success story however and we must plan for resilience for those days too.

Some individuals are blessed with the ability to compartmentalise their lives and can readily leave work and work related concerns at the office, hospital, surgery or practice. Others have a mental briefcase constantly with them. The baggage of work haunts them. It is impossible to change your personality it is said but recognising which type you fall into is important. It then allows more active management of the interface between work and the rest of your life. We all have different ways of relaxing. Exercise, the gym, jogging, swimming and running are quite common ways of defusing stress and re-energising ourselves. You will know what works for you. A note of caution however. It is good to talk and 'get stuff off your chest' but endless revisiting of work related issues can be really destructive in a home environment. Know when to stop.

Your mental and physical health is important to you and to your team and organisation. Look after yourself and look after them. They may need to talk round and about work related issues and this can be helpful in ensuring comfort with arrangements and mutual support. They in turn will look after you. This is a virtuous circle. Mutual respect is key.

Your family and friends do not want to lose sight of you when you take this role on. However stimulating it is for you to be a clinical leader their interest in you is at a warm human level. They want your time, your attention and to be the centre of your existence. You owe them and yourself that focus.

Don't be daunted by taking on a clinical leadership role but do go into it with your eyes (and ears) open. We all have something different to offer. Make sure your contribution is recognised and that you play to your strengths.

Take Home Messages

- **Look after yourself**
- **Ensure and plan for life work balance**

CHAPTER 20

Clinical Leaders: Heroes or Heretics?

This question was posed at the beginning of the book and we parked it.

It is probably clear now that perception is all. To some, as a clinical leader, you may be a hero. Most often that would be hero of the day, the meeting or the specific issue. To others you may be the heretic or the clinician who has jumped the fence to the dark side of management and sold out the profession. Whilst there are robust views on this topic it is often a matter of shifting sand. Trying for popularity is not a good idea. You can not please all of the people all of the time. Neither is it worth trying to. Being true to your own principles and maintaining your own integrity is important. Some days you are the pigeon and some days you are the statue. Colleagues may use and abuse your time and expertise. They mean nothing by this. They are just moving their own agenda forward. Be slow to take offence. You may be a juggler with multiple complicated issues and large agendas feeling that some days you are pleasing nobody, not even yourself. The satisfaction comes through working through the complex and making the service improvement or change. Transformation is never finished. It is a mind set and an on going process. The reward is personal fulfillment and satisfaction. It is important to enjoy the challenge of leadership, to learn and to move on. Tomorrow is always another day!